R. H. (Robert Henry) Newell

Smoked Glass

R. H. (Robert Henry) Newell

Smoked Glass

ISBN/EAN: 9783743301436

Manufactured in Europe, USA, Canada, Australia, Japa

Cover: Foto ©ninafisch / pixelio.de

Manufactured and distributed by brebook publishing software
(www.brebook.com)

R. H. (Robert Henry) Newell

Smoked Glass

BY
ORPHEUS C. KERR,
AUTHOR OF "ORPHEUS C. KERR PAPERS," "AVERY GLIBUN," ETC.

WITH ILLUSTRATIVE ANACHRONISMS BY THOMAS WORTH.

NEW YORK:
G. W. CARLETON, PUBLISHER.
LONDON: S. LOW, SON, & CO.
MDCCCLXVIII.

Entered, according to Act of Congress, in the year 1868, by
GEO. W. CARLETON,
In the Clerk's Office of the District Court for the Southern District of New York.

ROCKWELL & ROLLINS, STEREOTYPERS AND PRINTERS,
122 Washington Street, Boston.

CONTENTS.

	PAGE
VERBA SESQUIPEDALIA	9

LETTER I.

Narrating a pleasing Anecdote of New Jersey; describing the friendly Visit of an exciting Journalist to an able military Candidate for the Presidency; noting the disinterested Organization of the "Grand Mackerel Army of the Republic;" and giving the truly American Song and Story with which that Organization was partly celebrated,   17

LETTER II.

Illustrating, by a moral Connecticut Tale, the Fallacy of that political Inspiration which is derived from the Graves of great Men; picturing the solemn Impeachment of A. Johnson at the Bar of the Senate, and showing the great public Demoralization ensuing therefrom, ...   37

LETTER III.

Wherein our Correspondent not only introduces a fashionable Washingtonian Belle, but also audaciously takes Advantage of a Delay in Impeachment to address himself exclusively to the stylish young Maidens of the Period, ...   49

LETTER IV.

Explaining the surprising Equanimity of a Nation under complicated Misfortunes by the parallel Case of a great Philosopher of the Sixth Ward; confessing the inexplicable Levity produced by the honest Sentiments of a solid Boston Man; and celebrating the Grand Opening of the Theatre of War with the Spectacular Drama of Impeachment, ...   65

LETTER V.

Introducing an impecunious but loyal Southern Cavalier; depicting a gorgeous stage Procession in the mighty Spectacle of Impeachment; reporting the unexampled and convincing inaugural Argument of Manager Butler, and the visible Consternation of nervous Auditors thereat, ... 77

LETTER VI.

Which Attempts the sublime, but succeeds to a certain Extent only; yet quotes favorite Passages from the prevailing Drama as they are being simultaneously ground out, to great Applause, by "Organs" all about the Country, ... 88

LETTER VII.

Charging the Radicals with the continued and exasperating wet Weather; setting forth the great Wrong done to the Conservative Kentucky Chap; repeating a Conversation in the Boxes and Scene on the Stage of the Theatre of War; remarking the first of the Soliloquies for the Defence; and announcing a Visit from the direful "Ku-Klux Klan," 96

LETTER VIII.

Chanting an astonishing Lay in honor of clear Weather once more; irreverently likening the stately Abode of Congress to a Stomach; mentioning an attempted Speculation with Captain Samyule Samith, in real Estate, at Taikachor Court House; and sampling Andrew Nelson's Soliloquy, ... 107

LETTER IX.

Being a voracious Account of the unparalleled Match against Nature by the "American Proof-Reader" and the "Boston Marvel;" and its inevitably tragical Termination, ... 119

LETTER X.

Moralizing upon the certain Result of Vice-Presidency; giving the curious Epitaph of a victim of Eloquence; presenting the principal Gems of a Guano Matinée; and recording the Enthusiasm of the Populace over the last of the Impeachment Speeches, . . . 130

CONTENTS.

LETTER XI.

Taking a hopeful View of the Future of American Art; affording valuable Hints to the coming great Historical Painter; and showing how a sudden and unprecedented Outbreak of Morality caused a lamentable "Hitch" in the great final Transformation Scene of the majestic Drama of Impeachment, ... 140

LETTER XII.

Narrating the sudden Journey of our Correspondent and Others to the South on a Mission of Reconstruction; illustrating the usual Gymnastic Perils of American Railroad Travel; and portraying how the writer and Captain Villiam Brown, Eskevire, were received by a renowned Confederacy, ... 150

LETTER XIII.

Ushering in the Lady of the Chateau with all the Forms and Graces; introducing Croquet and one of its usual Results; and recording the direful Mistake of an unsuspecting Union Officer, . . . 163

LETTER XIV.

Chronicling the arrival of P. Penruthers as a Suitor; the ancient feudal Ceremonies thereat; and the dreadful Demeanor of the Nobility at the ensuing Banquet, ... 172

LETTER XV.

Citing an Incident of the Southern Postal Service; interpolating an Impeachment Note from Washington, and a vague Wordsworthian Parody; and "conservatively" touching upon the Presidential Nomination of the last Mackerel General by a classical Convention, 182

LETTER XVI.

Showing how a disloyal Telegraph did pervert and mispunctuate the Mackerel General's "Letter of Acceptance;" and spiritedly depicting the great Munchausen Hunt and its lamentable Ending, . 194

LETTER XVII.

Illustrating the tremendous extraneous Influence of large-sized Names; and describing the most passionate and contemptuous Love Scene ever beheld in fashionable Southern Society by a Yankee Varlet, 206

LETTER XVIII.

Casually explaining the unique Latin Motto of an ancient House; but chiefly devoted to a brilliant Chivalric Tournament, and showing how the Nobility and Gentry demeaned themselves on that knightly Occasion, ... 215

LETTER XIX.

Paying a handsome Tribute to Woman; introducing a Bride, and Preparations for the Bridal; giving the Origin and Plan of Chipmunk Cathedral; sketching a grand Southern Ritualistic Wedding; and showing how our Correspondent was once "up to Snuff," . . 225

LETTER XX.

Recording a Day's Excursion up the Potomac; analyzing a Strawberry Festival, and reporting some of the Orations at Susper College Commencement, ... 240

LETTER XXI.

Which dilates upon the military Mind as affected by Southern Experience; shows how a deserving Southern Unionist was fearfully and wonderfully tried by Mackerel Court-Martial; and explains how Captain Munchausen, being fully Reconstructed, sent Greetings to the United States of America, and terminated this eventful History, ... 249

APPENDIX, ... 259

SMOKED GLASS.

VERBA SESQUIPEDALIA.

"A FEW words by way of introduction," — as an author frequently remarks, with much native ease of manner, when about to astonish such weak-minded readers as peruse prefaces, with some pages of strictly moral information.

Instruction as to the finely subtle significance of certain passages in the appended work, which but for such explanation might seem to have no particular meaning at all, is, of course, the apparent purpose of those few words; but, in a majority of cases, it is their genuine intent to hint, very clearly, that the author of the book should not be ignominiously forgotten in the book itself, and that he takes this opportunity to step casually before the curtain of Chapter I., and be modestly surprised at the ensuing applause.

Having devised the sinister plan of inserting his signature a full score of times in the historical volume which is herewith submitted to the public at a remarkably low price, the present writer may forego the solemnity of such sentences as, "The more thoughtful reader scarcely need be told that the following pages have a deeper," etc. "Something beyond the mere frivolous amusement of an idle hour is intended by," etc. He may also venture to stop addressing "the reader" in terms (inasmuch as that poor-spirited title applies as well to editors, studious inmates of charitable institutions, and other persons, who never pay for books, as to the really solvent individual who patronizes the bookseller), and inscribe what he has here in store to the honest retail book-buyer.

As the honest retail book-buyer now scanning this page has, presumedly, committed himself beyond all redemption by paying for the volume beforehand, it is scarcely worth while to treat even him with any particular ceremony; and if the absence of any farther propitiatory phrases should happen to strike him as a sign of disrespect, he is hereby coldly authorized to get back his money — if he can. Nothing being certain in this world, however, and the failure of a high-handed outrage of the latter kind coming within the range of human possibilities, it is to be hoped, for the sake of his family, that he will not make a fool of himself in the event of ill success, but quietly submit to the inevitable and go on with his reading. He has the book, the bookseller will not take it back again; and if his bad temper thereat *must* have some vent, let him seize the first opportunity to recommend a similar purchase to his mother-in-law.

Not to trifle with the miserable man any longer, and supposing his possession of any intelligence whatever to be purely a matter of vague conjecture, let it be explained for his instruction, that when his superiors wish to behold an Eclipse of the Sun, or any other solar entertainment, without injury to their eyes, they use Glass which has been Smoked; and that this sensible medium of astronomical vision not only protects the human sight from harmful confusion of objects, but also presents to it the celestial luminary freed from all extraneous glare and rigidly reduced to his true proportions. Viewed through such a medium, the gorgeous, blazing sun, undergoing eclipse, looks lamentably like an apothecary's most lurid show-bottle suffering serious encroachment from a dinner-pot, and the revelation is calculated to impress feeble minds with the conviction that all is not sun that glitters. Taking his idea from the device and its popular effects, the author of the present volume has, for seven years past, studied a variety of our most dazzling national achievements through a piece of Smoked Glass, with results not less actually strengthening to the eye than astonishingly lessening to the brilliance and apparent magnitude of the military and political pageants surveyed. The ingenuous mind becomes positively confounded at the singularly minute proportions to which much of the most brilliant generalship, patriotism, and statemanship is reduced, when thus stripped of the refractions of partisan prejudice and journalism, and commended in its simple realities to the undazzled sight. To such pitifully small objects, indeed, are they often resolved by the process, that a record of them in relatively diminished terms might fail to make them visible at all; and, hence, to render them clearly perceptible to others, the recorder is compelled to magnify, or, as the critical cant goes, exaggerate them.

So far as Burlesque means Perversion or Distortion of facts, the pages of this book do not come properly under that name. The flaw in the iron of the boiler which holds the really great peril of future explosion is that which the magnifying glass only can detect; and the flaws in Patriotism and Statesmanship, which most seriously menace the stability of a nation, must be magnified (or exaggerated, if you will) to the capacity of popular vision, in order that they may be recognized in time. The writer has precipitated brilliant events and personalities, in Washington and in the South, through a carefully prepared piece of Smoked Glass, and then magnified the reduced precipitates only so much as was requisite to make their organic characteristics patent to the weakest sight. Thus, the pageant of Impeachment is truly given as the culminative scene of a feud between Representative THADDEUS Stevens and President ANDREW Johnson; the able and dexterous Opening Argument of Manager B. F. Butler is presented in its absolute meaning, rather than in its ostensible design; the pomp of the presiding Chief Justice is shown to have been coldly tolerated, rather than in any sense practically respected; the passiveness of the nation is shorn of its philosophical lustre and explained in its true significance; the patriotic vehemence of partisan journalism of to-day is set forth as it will be judged to-morrow; and the lame conclusion of the drama is attributed to a cause at least as credible and apparently logical as the one generally assigned for it. The same fidelity to concrete actuality may be asserted for the sketches of such representative sectional characters as Captain Villiam Brown, from cosmopolitan New York; the conservative, from Kentucky; the solid Boston man; the loyal Southern Munchausen, etc.; and if, in treating of the concentrative national life at Washington, the author has not felt at liberty to ignore the notorious local coloring which sometimes comes in bottles, he has, at least, involved it in a tenderness of phraseology which should not offend the most decorous.

Recalling the honest retail book-buyer to the stand, and once more sneering at his palpable stupidity in requiring so much prefatory explanation, it may be hinted, that the description of Reconstructional life in the Southern comic States, is intended as a logical sequel to the first half of the history. When not beheld through a piece of Smoked Glass, the South has hitherto presented an effulgence of lordly state and chivalry which few dreamed of attributing to the inordinate reflection and refraction of female novelists and heavy mortgages. Even before the rebellion, a well-smoked glass would have enabled the thoughtful observer to trace much over-dazzling to the latter; but now, the same medium diminishes a race of haughty cavaliers to a community of woefully attired impecuniaires, and reveals their growing eclipse by empty dinner-pots under the delays of Reconstruction. Only the other day, the writer received from a person signing himself "Lucius Natura" a curious anatomical drawing, of which the following is a fac-simile: —

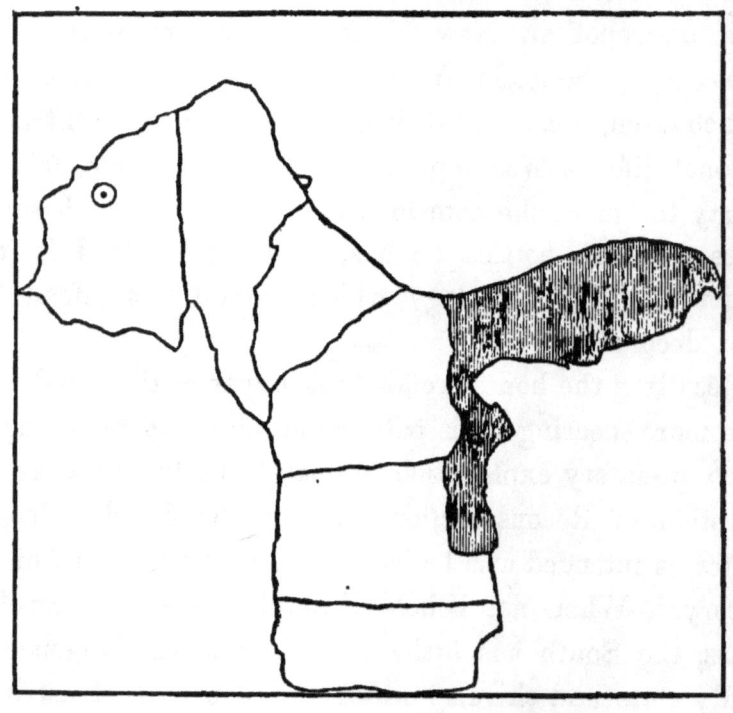

Accompanying which was a letter, wherein Lucius declared that a friend, in Georgia, had sent him from that State the fossil remain indicated by the *shaded part* of the drawing, and that, from thence, he (Lucius) had, by zoölogical induction, supplied other portions of the extinct animal. "My immediate impression," wrote Lucius, "was that the fossil (dug up in the extreme South, by-the-by) was nothing more than the hinder portions of some enormous dog (GENUS— *Caninus tremendibus*— Linnæus), which is represented by the symbol K. I.— a fallacy. I next assigned it to the Beaver tribe (GENUS— *Tilelus*— Buffon; or *Plugus*— Descartes; or, perhaps, *Nobus Coveræ*.) By unmistakable indications, I perceived that the animal was assimilated to the lowest *rodents*, which, says Cuvier, are possessed of the least intelligence of all.

"Goldsmith says: 'The beaver seems to be now the only remaining monument of brutal society. From the results of its labors, *which are still to be seen in the remote parts of America*, we learn how far instinct can be aided by imitation. We from thence perceive to what degree animals, without . . . . reason, can concur for their mutual advantage. . . . . When alone, the beaver has but little industry, ... and is without cunning sufficient to guard it against the most obvious and bungling snares laid for it.'

"In short, I am sure that my construction of the animal is correct, and that it belongs to the beaver tribe."

The present historian was much pleased with this triumph of the naturalist, and particularly admired the mild eye of the restored animal; but happening to think of his Smoked Glass, he quickly brought that to bear upon the drawing, and was astounded to discover that the reconstructed fossil was nothing more than a Map of Virginia, the Carolinas, Georgia, Florida, Alabama, and Mississippi, taken apart from the rest of the country and turned on end; and that the mild eye merely indicated the capitol of the first-named State.

From this, it will be perceived, that the Southern comic States have no protection from outrage, while Reconstruction, from whatever cause, is delayed. As the writer knows, from recent personal observation, through a proper medium, at Chipmunk Court House, they yearn eagerly for peace, and the withdrawal of our military vandals; they desire early investments of Northern Capital with them on good bond and mortgage; and, now that the fiercest gust of passion is over, the more advanced of them would even prefer the supremacy of the African, to being ruled, like us of the North, by the Corkasian.

O. C. K.

LETTER I.

NARRATING A PLEASING ANECDOTE OF NEW JERSEY; DESCRIBING THE FRIENDLY VISIT OF AN EXCITING JOURNALIST TO AN ABLE MILITARY CANDIDATE FOR THE PRESIDENCY; NOTING THE DISINTERESTED ORGANIZATION OF THE "GRAND MACKEREL ARMY OF THE REPUBLIC;" AND GIVING THE TRULY AMERICAN SONG AND STORY WITH WHICH THAT ORGANIZATION WAS PARTLY CELEBRATED

WASHINGTON, D. C., March 4, 1868.

Now that old Winter has been impeached, on charge of poking his snows into all manner of things, and despotically endeavoring to bring our whole excellent Republican organization to its sneeze; now that icicles, like D. Sickles, have ceased being hangers-on around the House, and gone to vapor all about the country; now that one in his goings can distinguish between his toes and froze, and get a little hoarse from some other cause than having caught colt; — it is pleasant to see fair Nature preparing to don her new Spring-bonnet for a promenade, and trying on a veil of fog now and then to study the effect; and it is also pleasant to travel, at this dustless season of the year, especially after you have passed beyond the limits of New Jersey.

Whoever has made the passage to this city, my boy, must have noticed that, soon after the starting of the train from New York, all the passengers became inexpressibly melancholy of visage, and devoted the most absorbing attention to the extreme backs of the hats on the next seat. If some innocent foreigner, or other emigrant, in the car, chanced (while hastily flying from the water-cooler under the impression that it was the boiler) to remark upon this freak of nature, the nearest native exclaimed, in a chilling whisper: "Hush! Mr. Hepworth Dixon,[*] hush! We are now passing through the State of Camden and Amboy, and if we look out of the windows we shall be CHARGED for it." Whereupon a deep shudder of terror ran through the entire vehicle, and Mr. Dixon made a memorandum in his note-book, to say, in his next exciting volume on "America," that the Jerseymen all had "Spiritual Wives," and allowed no through-passengers to look into their second-story windows, going-by, without paying for it.

Through being generally mistaken for the pig-pasture and cabbage-patch of New York, the arable Dutchy of New Jersey has not always received that amount of foreign notice which our more complacent editors delight to quote from the columns of engaging English journals; but the day will come — mark me, scoffer! — the day will come, when her name shall appear in every dictionary in the world — as a synonym for "Economy."

The vegetable interests of my dining-table made me acquainted, last summer, with a Jerseyman of innumerable

---

[*] Mr. Hepworth Dixon, of the London "Athenæum;" author of "New America," "Spiritual Wives," and other chaste works of imagination.

cucumbers; and, after recovering from the cholera which he had sold me at not more than the usual friendly percentage over the highest market-price, I went to his place to board, for the recovery of my health, at rather more per week than an own mother-in-law would have charged. He was a Jerseyman, full of deep love for nature, especially when she could be sold for so much a load, a basket, or a small measure; and was even so fond of animated creatures that he cheerfully encouraged all his neighbors to keep chickens, and buy corn for them from him. "And those sweet little English sparrows that are flying about now-a-days," says he to me, — "I love them because they are the works of my Maker; and I see that five hundred of them are advertised for, to be taken West, for which a reasonable sum would be paid. How can I encourage the pretty creeturs to flutter softly about my door?" Much moved by his beautiful enthusiasm, I suggested that a little bird-seed, placed upon a board, would attract the valuable warblers. He smiled feebly at me, and says he: "The seed would cost something, and I'm afeared they'd eat it. I suppose you haven't got a little seed about you, that you'd let me have, without wanting it deducted from your board?" Of course I had not; and for a whole week that admirer of the feathered works of his Maker was a mournful man. Suddenly, however, he brightened again amazingly; and early one morning, when an astounding twittering had called me to the front of the house, I found him cheerfully laughing to himself under a board upon a window-sill, around which some scores of sparrows were making much melody. "What!" exclaimed I, "have you really bought the seed at last, and put it on the sill? How could you afford it?" He caught me by the lappel of my coat, and slapped his leg, gleefully; and says he: "H'sh—sh! don't speak so that they can hear. There's some seed up there, to be sure; BUT I'VE GLUED IT FAST TO THE BOARD!"

Perhaps I should not have remembered the circumstance, but for the fact that the representative of that same gentleman's district in Congress is about to present his State's retraction of her former assent to the only civilized Constitutional Amendment* we have had in a year. Some States go too far to the Republican extreme, and some too far to the Democratic; but you must look to New Jersey, if you would find the golden "mean."

Pondering this reminiscence en route, I succeeded in reaching the Capital without experiencing that unnatural disposition to mid-day slumber, which generally attends the intervening approach to Philadelphia on the way. Philadelphia produces some very creditable firemen, and will probably be a quite lively place when the final conflagration of things occurs; but, in the mean time, it curiously resembles some of those placid California fruits, which will keep growing larger and larger just so long as you choose to leave them alone, and are seldom troubled

---

* The Fourteenth Amendment.

with enough distinctive flavor to tell whether they are ordinary pumpkins, or extraordinary apples.

Once again established in Washington, and in my old room at Willard's, I find little of merely local importance to note immediately, save, perhaps, the number of former Southern confederacies, who daily haunt the White House of our reigning sovereign, A. Johnson, *Rex tailoronis*, and take numerous Pardons at his expense. These haughty noblemen are quite affable once more in general society, and seem ready to negotiate fresh mortgages even with rich reptiles from New England; yet it cannot be denied that they still look with eyes of fire upon such of our national vandals in military attire as they chance to behold around the War Office.

But if the well-known Southern Confederacy has reason to feel more or less indignation against our former strategic national troops for exploding the incendiary musket against her, she may find much inexpressible comfort, my boy, in contemplating the dreadful retribution now visited upon the head of the last General of the Mackerel Brigade by the pleasing emissaries of an incorrigible daily press. The other day, an affable and exhaustive correspondent of one of our more exciting morning journals, having learned that the General was under orders to become President of the United States in 1869, went cheerfully to his private residence to make inquiries concerning his character, and ascertain his views of the freed-negro race. Reaching the chamber of the great man, where the latter sat practising upon the accordion, this gifted and friendly correspondent first glanced over two or three private letters, which were lying upon a desk near the window, and then says he, —

"Although attached to a journal which gains ten thousand in circulation per week, I am inclined to regard you as an equal, and shall only publish such portions of your correspondence with your family as may be interesting to our female readers. I find here," says he, opening a drawer in the desk, and smiling agreeably, "a penknife, with which I will pare my nails, while asking you such questions as the nation is determined to have answered. Firstly: What is your income for the current year, and how is your grandmother's sprained ankle?"

The veteran attentively regarded the middle knuckle of his right hand, and performed "Ever of Thee," on the accordion.

"I see," went on this cheerful correspondent, "that your servant has just brought in your breakfast, and I don't know but I *will* try one of those eggs myself. While I am eating I shall trouble you to tell me what you spend a year for clothes, and also what property your wife brought you. The people of the country are naturally anxious to have these matters clearly explained at once, and any equivocation will tend only to depreciate our bonds abroad, and disappoint a legitimate curiosity at home."

The great soldier fixed his glance earnestly upon a spot

near the middle of the ceiling, and executed "Oh, ask me not," with dreamy effect.

"I will try one of your cigars, for a change," said the able correspondent, going to the box on the shelf; "and while I am looking for a match in the pocket of that waistcoat of yours, hanging on that nail, you might tell me how many marriageable nieces you have; and also, how much you contribute toward the support of your unmarried aunt. The general public will scarcely be satisfied with anything but the most direct replies to these queries; and if you will also inform me what you gave for your last dozen of shirts, I shall feel obliged."

The hero now took a deep interest in the left-hand corner of the table near him, and softly evolved, "Come, rest in this Bosom," from his eloquent instrument of music.

"You are doubtless quite ready," continued this engaging correspondent, abstractedly dressing his hair with a comb and brush from the bureau, "to state how much you allow your wife for keeping house, and how much you expect to make this year. Upon these points, of course, your fellow-countrymen expect explicit information; nor must I forget to ask how you stand regarding the extension of suffrage to the freed-negro race?"

Here the famous veteran slowly arose from his chair, carefully laid his accordion upon the table, and — winked. Then he quietly lifted a cat from the floor, deliberately blew a ridge in her fur, and dexterously extracted therefrom, with thumb and finger, an agile triumph of the insect kingdom. Thus supplied, he advanced upon the affable and exhaustive correspondent, led him smilingly to the door by an arm, delicately deposited the insect in his right ear, and closed the interview.

And this subject naturally leads me to consider the "Grand Mackerel Army of the Republic," which was organized here on Tuesday evening, by certain officers of the great strategic Brigade, and the inaugural meeting of which I had the honor to attend. The organization is for the purpose of promoting the Presidency of the above General, keeping alive the memory of those feats of arms and legs, without which we should not now be on hand as a nation, and securing for the most strategical officers of our late forces that marked political recognition so necessary to persons who propose becoming governors, postmaster, or successful clergymen. The meeting was held in the immediate neighborhood of a bar-room; so that, in case of fire, water might be readily attainable; and I was pleased to exchange greetings once more with Captains Villiam Brown and Samyule Sa-mith, Sergeant O'Pake, and the thoughtful Mackerel Chaplain.

The object of the organization having been stated by a waiter, and the memory of those of our comrades who have married since the war having been drank in silence, the next toast in order was, —

"Our Native Land."

To this Sergeant O'Pake responded. He said that our

Native Land was open to all Irishmen, whether they came from Italy, Poland, or Hungary; and that even to Americans it offered some advantages. When we spoke of our Native Land, however, we particularly meant the refuge of the foreign martyr of freedom; of him who believed that Man *must* be Free, no matter what he was indicted for, and never hesitated to break jail in demonstration of that immortal truth. He — the speaker — could not better answer the last toast, than by presenting a rhythmical statement of the woes of the general foreign refugee of Freedom; and, while giving the body of the sad tale in Irish, that it might seem more like home to Americans, he had also sufficiently flavored the strain with various foreign tongues to make it suit the general and everlasting martyr of tyranny. He begged leave, therefore, to recite, —

THE UNIVERSAL EXILE'S LAMENT.

Attind to me, mother, while loud I'm complaining,
   And bend your swate eyes more complately to hear;
For weakness of voice is just all I am gaining,
   Locked up in a jail, with no comrade to cheer.
Ye'll say it's from jail that I'm always a-writing,
   Ah, true is the story — *pieta di me!*
And now, as before, what has caused my indicting
   Is just my insisting, that
          Man MUST be free!

But twinty years old was my age as I reckon,
   When one of my friends had his landlord to pay;
And quick we agreed, o'er a bottle of whiskey,
   To settle the rint with shillalies in play.

It's somebody's head that I cracked in a jiffy, —
  My own sunny France, I was striking for thee ! —
And straight to a prison *les tyrans* conveyed me,
  Despite my protesting that
            Man MUST be free !

I served like a baste through my period penal,
  Wi' a' the composure auld Reekie inspires ;
And spake to the judge in his altitude venal,
  As one in whose bosom were liberty's fires.
Then home I repaired ; but, before I got thither,
  A bit of a mob made me join in their glee ;
It's government houses we burned, and some people,
  To prove we were drunk, and that
            Man MUST be free !

Myself did they take, with some dozens of others,
  And gave us a trial for trayson indade ;
And sintinced us all, right in sight of our mothers,
  To cross the wide ocean with fetters and spade.
Not *ein hohes wort* was in all of their charges :
  But stern was the Justice, and, " Pris'ner," says he,
" How came you to join in this burning and stealing ? "
  " To show," says I, boldly, " that
            Man MUST be free ! "

When safely arrived at the scene of our labors,
  I found the Commandant quite gintly inclined ;
He singled me out from the midst of my neighbors,
  And softly I gave him a piece of my mind :
" I'm sickly," says I, " and have nade of indulgence,
  Nor will I abuse it if given to me."
He trusted my word and indulged me, *per Baccho*,
  And soon I escaped, because
            Man MUST be free !

Then straight to this country I fled for protection,
  And wasn't I hailed as a patriot born ?

They asked me to stand for a local election, —
  But such a small offer I treated with scorn.
And soon did I join, with an energy aygur,
  Some gintlemen proud as it's aisy to be,
Who went into fighting for keeping the naygur,
  And showing, *per Dio,* that
            Man MUST be free!

Bad luck to it all! 'twas a bating they gave us,
  And *Allah il Allah!* was all I could say;
From starving down South there was nothing to save us
  And I was not slow about coming away:
It's not for a pardon I'd ask of the rulers,
  Nor yet would I seek from the country to flee;
For what could they do in a real republic
  To one who said only that
            Man MUST be free!

Not troubled at all in me mind for the morrow,
  I turned my attintion to matters of State;
And so, having failed, to my infinite sorrow,
  In fighting the nation, took comfort of fate.
'Twas right in the midst of advising the rulers
  Just how they should act to the South, and to me, —
When "*Credat Judæus!*" they say; and I'm taken
  To jail, though explaining that
            Man MUST be free!

Sure, mother, but Liberty's all a delusion,
  And Italy, Hungary, Poland, and I,
Can only be kept in eternal confusion
  By hoping for landlords and despots to die.
So, here let me say, in the musical tongue of
  My own native Venice — *Venite per me!*
It's most of me time that I'm spending in prison,
  And all from insisting that
            Man MUST be free!

After we had all applauded the touching verses as well as our tears of sympathy would permit, and expressed our sincere regret that we could not all be Irishmen, the next toast was offered, —

"The Last General of the Mackerel Brigade — Our next President."

As I had been selected to honor this sentiment, and really knew no presidential qualification that the General possessed, save his well-known fondness for horse-flesh (and consequent supposable understanding of the common wheel), I merely paid a passing tribute to his skill with the accordion, and related a story of that horse-y State,

VERMONT.

Possibly you have never happened to hear of such a town as Twinkleton before; and so I am careful to state that it is within sound of the whistle of the train that "breaks-up" at Bellows Falls, Vermont, and that its principal hotel for man and beast is somewhat afflictive to the digestions of those travellers whose stomachs look upon apple-pie three times a day as something in the nature of a persecution. You say to the stage-driver, at the railway station, that you wish to go to Twinkleton; and, if you happen to wear a scarf-pin with the head of a coral horse upon it, he will induce you, by a series of the most ingenious devices, to distrust the comfort of the "insides," and ride upon the box with him.

"You're going to buy a horse up there," says he, turning the reins in his hand, and glancing from your scarf-pin to your city hat.

"No, sir!" you say, rather sharply; for you have an idea that you look vastly above anything horsey, and wish your general get-up to be considered impressive.

"Well, then," says the driver, "of course you must be going to 'Squire Maple's; so there's no use of my talking to you abaout that ere nigh-pacing mare, I s'pose."

He can't conceive the possibility, can't the driver, of any other destination for you in Twinkleton than 'Squire Maple's; and you instinctively feel that a request on your part to be put down at any other mansion, or at the hotel, would at once entail upon you the suspicion of coming to buy a horse secretly, and subject you to some pretty heavy boring in regard to the nigh-pacing mare.

Such a state of things will seem to indicate that no masculine visitor to Twinkleton is safe from buying a horse, unless he stops at 'Squire Maple's. This is true; and I defy any unarmed single gentleman of my acquaintance to pass a night in Twinkleton without having a steed forcibly sold to him by somebody before morning. In a wider sense, it will seem to indicate that 'Squire Maple's is *the* mansion of Twinkleton. This also is true, and makes me quite anxious to lead my friends thither without further preface.

Taking upon ourselves mantles of invisibility, we boldly enter the hospitable door of this celebrated house, and are quite surprised to find host, hostess, daughters, and a young-man visitor named young Mr. Blinders, very heartily welcoming that delicious specimen of a girl who came up in the stage with us.

"My dear Maggie Pye," say both of the old folks at once, "we're *so* glad to see you. How *did* you leave pa and ma? Mr. Blinders, this is our niece from New York, Miss Pye."

Young Mr. Blinders ducks his head with great emotion, turns very red in the face, and puts both of his hands still deeper into his pockets.

A smile of rather cruel amusement is beginning to curl brightly from the corners of Miss Pye's charming mouth, when her cousins, Cassandra and Minerva, commence to tear off her "things," like affectionate young wild-cats, and she permits Mr. Blinders to go uncrushed for the nonce.

Questions, answers, and hugs run riot for ten minutes; after which there is a hasty washing of hands and smoothing of locks, and then dinner is officially announced by a young woman who has seen better days, — or, at least, days when there would not be so many plates to wash.

The table is substantially and generously furnished, though, perhaps, the presence of doughnuts as an *entrée* and apple-pie as a vegetable, might not be considered orthodox in Fifth Avenue. It is a table to make one feel at a glance that the natural act of eating is a plain, honest, hearty act, not to be entered upon with any mawkish pretences of bird-like pecking. Down they all sit, and the 'squire helps to corned pork and doughnuts all around; after which delicate operation he starts up the talk.

"Well, Maggie, did you have a nice ride up? I wonder whether George drove the roans, or the grays, to-day?"

"The roans — I seen 'em."

This from young Mr. Blinders, who is immediately conscious of having committed an indiscretion, and knocks over a tumbler of water with his elbow by way of helping matters.

"Is George the driver's name?" says Maggie. "Why! don't you think, uncle, he thought I was coming to Twinkleton to buy a horse, and confidentially offered to sell me a pacing mare!"

"O Cassandry!" says Minerva, appealing to her sister, "only think of Mag's buying a horse out of her own pocket!"

He! he! from Minerva, to accompany the ha! ha! of 'Squire Maple, to accompany the hor! hor! hor! of young Mr. Blinders.

"Well, I tell you what it is, girls," says Maggie, shaking her curls; "pa's given me a hundred dollars to spend, and I'm more than half a mind to buy a dear angel of a saddle-horse with it. I do love horseback riding so much, and our coupé horses aint fit."

"I say, Miss Pye —"

This from young Mr. Blinders, whose speech is suddenly checked by a nudge from Miss Minerva, and a magical removal of his pocket-handkerchief from the table to his pocket.

"Ah, Maggie, my girl," says the 'squire, "I consider myself responsible for you now, and shan't let you run through your fortune in that way."

Miss Pye is about to respond with some playful defiance, when she is surprised at receiving a most sinister and complicated wink from the right eye of young Mr. Blinders.

The impudent booby! she thinks. How dare he! But she is too good-natured to take serious offence, and begins to plan some choice fun at his expense.

Dinner is over, and young Mr. Blinders lingers around the room in speechless clumsiness until the chatter becomes deafening, when he springs convulsively from his chair, makes a gape at Miss Pye, as though about to utter something remarkable, and then goes home.

Thereupon his peculiarities are all picked to pieces, as are those of all gentlemen who have just left the company of ladies; and Miss Maggie Pye rollickingly avows that she has made a conquest of him already, and intends to do him brown. The Misses Cassandra and Minerva make a show of defending him; but the general conclusion is, that he was born expressly to be made an example of for the warning of all presumptuous young men. It is nearly eleven o'clock, P. M., when the question is finally settled, and then all the little dears retire to a double-bedded dormitory upstairs, and in a vivacious discussion of the Fashions talk themselves delightfully to sleep.

Next day young Mr. Blinders comes to dinner again, and lingers through the afternoon, and manages to ask Miss Pye, in a blood-curdling whisper, if she is "going to be scared out of it by them Mapleses?"

In utter bewilderment Maggie is about to come out with a Good gracious me! when young Mr. Blinders abruptly bolts out of the house, and leaves subsequent laughter to serve as a flattering comment on his fragmentary style of wooing. Oh, such a goose!

On the following morning, however, he comes not long after breakfast, when the Misses Cassandra and Minerva — whose excellent parents *will* pronounce their names as though spelled with a final *y* — artfully manage to leave Miss Pye alone in the dining-room with him.

Five minutes, — ten minutes, — fifteen minutes, — and the front door is heard to close after somebody, and Miss Pye comes tearing upstairs to the girls' room with her curls fairly on end.

"O Cassy and Minny!" says she, "it's too funny! What do you think? He's asked me to elope with him, and I've agreed!"

"What!"

"Yes! Says he to me, 'I say, Miss Pye, you aint a going to be watched and governed by these Mapleses — be ye?' Of course I told him 'No!' And then says he — oh, dear, it's too funny, though! — says he, 'Then all you've got to do is to meet me out at the road-gate tonight after the Mapleses is abed, and then we'll take the liberty of doing as we please, with our own horse and our own money.' Now, girls, we must keep up the fun, you know; and I want both of you to hide behind those two poplars down by the gate to-night and hear me rig your country beau."

The Misses Cassandra and Minerva are at first disposed to decline any part in such a conspiracy; but remember in time that they have been called "these Mapleses" as well as their parents, and determine to witness the downfall.

Night comes; seven o'clock; eight o'clock, ma goes to bed; nine o'clock, pa says he must go to bed; ten o'clock, and pa *does* go to bed. Half-past ten o'clock, and the Misses Cassandra and Minerva are behind the poplars, and Miss Pye is at the appointed gate. In five minutes thereafter young Mr. Blinders suddenly emerges from the dense shade of two trees across the road, and cautiously approaches the wicket.

"I say, Miss Pye!" in a whisper.

"Well, sir," responds Maggie, timidly, quite alarmed for a moment as the magnitude of her joke flashes upon her.

"Shall we go to him, or shall I bring him here?" whispers young Mr. Blinders, with great self-possession.

He means the clergyman, thinks Miss Pye. I ought to be ashamed of myself to fool the poor fellow so, I declare; but I'll put him out of his misery at once, and as delicately as I can.

"No, Mr. Blinders," she says, "I cannot go with you. In an affair of this kind my parents should be consulted—"

"I say, Miss Pye," interrupts young Mr. Blinders, "it's only them Mapleses that could come between us in this, and it aint none of their business, anyhow. All I ask is the hundred dollars that old Maples wanted to be responsible for, you know?"

"Sir!" says Miss Pye, horror-stricken at such mercenary frankness.

"Just let me show him to you, you know. I've got him nigh under that tree over there," says young Mr. Blinders, incoherently.

"Him? What *do* you mean?" shrieks Miss Pye.

"Mean?" says young Mr. Blinders, "why, just the very saddle-horse for your hundred dollars."

"I thought you wanted to run away with me!" screamed Miss Pye, quite forgetting herself.

There is a sound in the air as of the emphatic naming of a Holy City of the Orient; in fact, the emphasized syllables are those of "Jerusalem!" and a manly form is seen in the faint moonlight to make rapid strides across the road.

"Tch — tch — tch — he! he! he!" comes from one poplar tree inside the gate.

"Tch — tch — tch — te-he! te-he!" comes from behind another poplar tree inside the gate.

Two plump female shapes come from behind two poplar trees inside the gate and surround a third female shape, while a swift horseman clatters furiously past the *outside* of the gate, and disappears.

O Miss Pye! Miss Margaret Pye! how *are* you now, my pretty dear? "What's this? Where are you?" Why, this is the hand of your Cousin Minerva trying to pour some more water into your mouth; and you are in — VERMONT!

At the termination of this jockeylar story in honor of the known equineinity of the subject of the toast, there was much hearty laughter by everybody except those beside myself; but the hilarity was both general and unseemly when I subsequently spoke in terms of glowing eulogy concerning one whose sterling worth was yet to be acknowledged; whose qualification for the most renumerative office could not be questioned; and whose name — said I — is   ORPHEUS C. KERR.

LETTER II.

ILLUSTRATING, BY A MORAL CONNECTICUT TALE, THE FALLACY OF THAT POLITICAL INSPIRATION WHICH IS DERIVED FROM THE GRAVES OF GREAT MEN; PICTURING THE SOLEMN IMPEACHMENT OF A. JOHNSON, AT THE BAR OF THE SENATE, AND SHOWING THE GREAT PUBLIC DEMORALIZATION ENSUING THEREFROM.

WASHINGTON, D. C., March 12, 1868.

As we survey Old Age, my boy, through a piece of Smoked Glass, and observe its impressive use of colored silk handkerchiefs; as we note how much respectability it can express in a sonorous cough, and how much knowledge of our own inmost thoughts and insignificant youthfulness it can impress upon us with the gleam of its remorseless spectacles, — as we survey and note these things, I say, we must indeed feel inspired with abject reverence for all that is past sixty, and refuse to consider a scratch-wig and gold-headed cane in any way detrimental to the hoary majesty of the patriarch.

But if these mere externals of benignant longevity make us feel, by comparison, like superfluous babes, what tender sensations lift the soft mist of nature's distillations to our eyes, when we see the tranquil hearts of the old clinging one to another in a friendship as deep and quiet as the long sleep in which they must soon be still! By that intuitive sympathy which makes natural friends of all men when they stand together upon the verge of a land equally strange to all, the withered hand clasps strong the withered hand on the borders of an unexplored Eternity.

In a village, on the blue Connecticut, where young shad are salted and sold for the best No. 1 Mackerel, and negro suffrage is considered an insidious device of federal tyranny, — in this Arcadian hamlet, where innocence exists to a degree that is oppressive to the senses, — I once knew two venerable men, whose friendship for each other I have never seen equalled, save by that of Secretary Seward for the Czar of Russia. For years they had peregrinated together in this vale of tears, until they actually became as like as brothers, even in physical aspect. The nose of one had the same caloric hue with the nose of the other. The breath of one exhaled the aroma of a liquid of the tropical isles, only to exactly counterfeit the West Indian fragrance labiated by the other. Even in the management of their tumblers they were like a man and his glass; and one, who remembered having seen them sober once (when they were children), said that they seemed much drawn together whenever they got into the same wagon.

At last one of them died suddenly of a distracted panorama of black monkeys, and was placed in the village graveyard, under a stone bearing the simple Latin inscription "Hic!"

The survivor uttered no lamentations; his only words

for a week were but reiterations of the one syllable of his friend's epitaph; yet he shed tears to an extent which (inasmuch as he never touched water) made his frequent falls the evident result of "drop"-sy. One night, while returning in great mental anguish from a protracted interview with the glass-clerk of the village hotel, he was attacked with great violence by both sides of the road, and driven irregularly into the wayside inclosure where rested his ancient friend. And upon that friend's grave did he sadly stretch himself; nor was the touching pathos of the act lessened by his simple-hearted belief that he was retiring to bed at home, nor by his broken utterance of the word,—

"Wairzerquilt?"

At morn they found him there, roused him from his slumber, and rudely dragged him before the 'squire.

"What is the matter with you?" asked the latter.

The bereaved old man leaned heavily upon a constable for support, under his emotion, and said solemnly,—

"Isht'zfriendship."

"And is it friendship, too, which makes you speak in that thick way?" queried the 'squire.

"Yeshir," murmured the aged mourner,— "Yeshir!"

"I am afraid," added the magistrate, "that you are intoxicated."

The venerable prisoner smiled seraphically; but, happening to remember himself, he immediately frowned terribly. Then he smiled very violently again, and laid himself more comfortably upon the constable. After which, he repeated his friend's epitaph several times — with tears.

"Noshir," said he, — "noshir!"

"How, then, does it happen," went on the 'squire, "that you are found in your present condition?"

"Condizh'n?" ejaculated the venerable Damon, forming his lips suddenly into the shape of a very tight rose, and swaying majestically — "Condizh'n? Did you know my fren', shir? He was a drink'nman. Yeshir! — an' I caught it from siz-siz-szleepin' on's grave!"

I was reminded of this small and excellent Connecticut tale on Wednesday morning last, when the Venerable Gammon laid bare his benignant heart to such inalienable worshippers as had just invited him to take a brevet with them at the bar of Willard's Hotel.

"My children," said the aged benefactor of the universe, smiling mournfully at the boiled slice of lemon which he was about to swallow from a goblet, "my children, when I compare the Union of to-day with the Union formed by my old friend, George Washington, I feel that the present is not the past, and that the abyss toward which we are drifting is the chasm whither our footsteps tend. If to feel thus is to be disloyal," said the Venerable Gammon, with much oily effulgence of double-chin, "then was the male parent of his country disloyal; for I breathe but the warning spirit of the great Sleeper at Mount Vernon." Whereupon everybody admitted that Washington was, indeed, rather less ruinous than our present sagacious

Congress to everything national whatsoever; and it was proposed to present an immediate service of plate to the friend of the *Pater patria.*

It is sweet and soothing to know, my boy, that those who, by virtue of inexpressibly superior years, or recent political snubblings, are placed upon the particular watch-towers of the country, — it is sweet and soothing, I say, to know, that vigilant watchers like those, can detect coming Ruin at such a very long distance; that we are allowed plenty of time to avert it if we choose — by letting them ruin us beforehand.

Thinking of this, I was upon the point of leaving the place, when a Republican chap of much forehead called for another brevet, and says he, —

"The Union of to-day has been turned into a howling wilderness of irredeemable paper money by the presidential treachery of our former tailor. Men and brethren!" exclaimed this earnest chap, wildly; "it is Andrew Johnson who has wrought this inexpressible woe, which nothing but Impeachment can allay. To call him a demagogue were flattery. What, then, shall we call this man of sin?"

"Ah!" says a soft voice, "couldn't we call him a Sinagogue?"

Turning quickly, to see what creature was capable of such an unseemly suggestion at this solemn crisis in the history of our beloved country, I beheld Captain Villiam Brown, who, having recently returned from a meeting of

4*

the "Mackerel Army of the Republic," was on his way to assure Congress that our late strategic national troops may be depended upon in an emergency.

"Hail to thee, my son of swords," said I, affably. "Does Mars call again to deeds of high emprise; or come you hither only to be appointed Secretary of War *ad interim?* " *

"Ad interim!" says Villiam, dreamily. "No, my fren'; the military being who is too ready for an ad interim, only invites everybody to pitch interim; and when so many beings are pitchers, it is only left for him to be a tumbler. Impeachment," says Villiam, reasoningly, "is chiefly a matter of pitchers and tumblers — the former of which contain so much small-beer, that they will be found foaming at the mouth at the 'bar' of the Senate when the Sinagogue of the White House goes thither for his bitters."

Perceiving that Villiam's thirsty military mind mistook for a spirituous dispensary the august "bar" of that higher branch of our national legislature which has Ben Wade in the balance and is found wanting the Presidency, I led him out for a walk on the Avenue; and was about explaining to him that said bar offered nothing stronger than the occasional crusty port of Mr. Sumner, when we

* Despite the President's conciliating brevets, the appointment of Secretary of War *ad interim* fairly went begging amongst the military believers in its illegality, until finally an unbelieving THOMAS was found.

were abruptly accosted by a hasty Western chap in a soft black hat, linen duster, and gray worsted mittens.

"Excuse me," says he, pantingly; "but I have just arrived from the loyal State of Illinois to offer ten thousand muskets to Congress for its approaching single combat with the criminal tailor of the White House, and wish to be directed to the proper authorities."

"Ah!" says Villiam, "are they needle-guns?"

"Why should they be that kind?" says the chap, anxiously.

"Because," says Villiam, thoughtfully, "the President, being a tailor by profession, will naturally adopt the needle-gun for himself, in case of war. You know," says Villiam, pleasantly, "when there are breeches between two parties, and they come to be much wore, the 'needle' gun is likely to be most useful in patching up a piece."

The Western chap scowled, and says he, "I'm a gunmaker myself, and wish to sell the guns I have mentioned without further confusion." And he left us in great indignation.

"Behold," says Villiam, gazing after him, and simultaneously eating a clove — "behold, my fren', how the loyal heart of the country responds when a patriotic Congress stands forth against the *ad interim* of arbitrary tyranny. I really believe," says Villiam, confidently, "that if it should come to violence we might have every old duck-gun in the country — for cash."

Deeply impressed by the profound remark, I left him;

and in two hours thereafter was standing within the storied Senate-Chamber of the United States of America! I am not a bad man, my boy; nor can I accuse myself of any greater detriment to self-respect than may have been involved in the spending of several days in New Jersey without compulsion; but when I beheld that High Court of Impeachment, — when I looked down from the gallery upon that scene of much shirt-collar, tremendous forehead, and frequent judicial stomach, I was immediately conscious of the same painful insignificance I had felt once before in my life when surveying an Elephant. Upon that earlier occasion I strove to reason with myself against such humiliating personal microscopicality. I said to myself, there is unquestionably a certain aggravating LARGENESS about him, and if he wore proportionate spectacles and watch-seal he'd look nearly as majestic as a German musician. But where's the Mind — the giant human Mind! — to inform that vast tabernacle of flesh, and give those broad temples an equivalent intelligence?

It was of no use. I'd seen too many fat ones of my own kind, without minds, while attending the New York Constitutional Convention. I continued to feel smaller and smaller in that enormous presence, until it suddenly recurred to me that I had paid twenty-five cents to see the Immensity! At the thought, all my natural complacency came back in a flash! Yes, sir, I swelled immediately; and winked so much to myself, that an aged maiden in the throng thought herself affectionately addressed thereby, and dedicated a "personal" to me in next day's "Herald."

I shall not attempt to explain just why such a matter should affect me thus; but as I surveyed the High Court of Impeachment, and experienced the very same old sensation of comparative nothingness, I felt that the trouble lay in my not having paid twenty-five cents before entering. Going back, therefore, for a moment, I fairly compelled a doorkeeper to restore my self-respect by accepting the proper money, and was then in a condition to behold with some equanimity one of the most immense scenes in the history of our distracted globe.

A door opened; the Sergeant-at-arms advanced toward the Chair of the Senate, announcing "A Committee from the House of Representatives," and was followed by the Committee, headed by a very old man. The President of the Senate arose. It was proclaimed that any one who uttered sound from the galleries should be imprisoned. The Old Man — a very old man, and tottering; yet young and of granite, with the yearless, inexorable purpose of a Fate — handed his whip * to the Sergeant-at-arms, cast his hat upon a chair, and — paused. The President of the Senate glanced slowly around at the pale, intent faces about and above him; extended a hand aloft; and dropped a pin. The noise of the fall reached every ear distinctly. Then the Old Man spoke, —

---

* A mistake. It was not a whip, but a cane. — Ed.

"We, the Representatives of the Republic, in the name of the whole People of the United States, do Impeach Andrew Johnson, President of the United States, for certain High Crimes and Misdemeanors; and shall present, in substantiation thereof, divers Articles, known by grammar as the Definite and the Indefinite. And we do demand that the Senate take my order to call the said Andrew Johnson before its bar."

The President of the United States said: "The Senate will take that order;" and the Old Man (whose name, as I am informed, is Thaddeus Stevens) led his Committee in silence from the chamber.

It had been a grand, momentous, dreadful scene; and only the first, too, in a drama which were paralyzing to a nation not already schooled to tragedy in its high places. Who can wonder that it has already — it and its kind — produced much demoralization?

For instance: an enterprising chap of much news-agency has just been detected in a fraud possible only in a time of lax public morals, and unseemly ingenuity.

Having invented a means of skilfully changing the day and date of a newspaper at will, this unscrupulous chap has been distributing the very same copy of that excellent morning journal, The New York "Tribune," day after day to his patrons, for several months; buying it back for quarter-price each night, and dealing it out again to the same parties next morning with altered date-line. Probably he might have gone on thus for a year without detection, but for the recent discovery of a joyous man who had just forwarded a paid advertisement of the death of his mother-in-law, and had his suspicions aroused by not finding it in print.

A still sadder case is that of a thoughtful and venerable file who, being a subscriber for the New York "Times," had drawn two parallel but distinct chalk lines on the floor of his office, the one marked "Republican" and the other "Democratic." It was the custom of this truly eccentric file to stand upon one or the other of these lines when reading his favorite and admirable journal of a morning, according as that journal changed sides in politics each twenty-four hours; but it happened that when Impeachment became a fixed fact, the same pleasing daily journal took both sides with great ability.

The aged file tried thereupon to read with one foot on one line and the other on the other. Alas! the stretch was too great for one of his years, and he speedily became what is called "cracked." Then with the dread fires of insanity blazing in his eyes, he flew to the White House, tore madly into the presence of the President, fell upon his knees, and says he,—

"A boon! my liege, a boon!"

Mr. Johnson laid aside a spoon, the metal of which he had been testing in a glass retort containing some hot liquid preparation, and asked, "What can your lawful suzerain do for you, good Lorenzo? But hold! let me ring for an ad interim, or a brevet, to raise your spirits."

"No, my suzerain, I am not thirsty," cried the aged maniac. "But I would have your consent to wed an old lady in your employ, whom I love."

"Her name — what is it?" cried his sovereign, hastily.

"She is Secretary Welles, of the Navy," moaned the madman.

"Here, guards!" called the great ruler; "away with this lunatic. I would be alone."

This, this, is indeed Impeachment.

And now, my boy, as I close this letter, there comes news of the arrival of a high-toned Democrat of much cheek-bones, from New York, who, finding the carrying-in-coal profession rather dull just now, has sped hither to pledge ten thousand men for the support of the President against a demoniac Congress. But I smile softly to myself while I write, that no such needless aid will be accepted; for Mr. Johnson is a man who, under no possible provocation, could be induced to "take the 'Pledge.'"

Yours, unimpeachably,
ORPHEUS C. KERR.

LETTER III.

WHEREIN OUR CORRESPONDENT NOT ONLY INTRODUCES A FASHIONABLE WASHINGTONIAN BELLE, BUT ALSO AUDACIOUSLY TAKES ADVANTAGE OF A DELAY IN IMPEACHMENT TO ADDRESS HIMSELF EXCLUSIVELY TO THE STYLISH YOUNG MAIDENS OF THE PERIOD.

WASHINGTON, D. C., March 20, 1868.

WHAT luxury of feeling there is in that earliest hour of recognized Spring, when the door by which Winter has gone out can be left open for a while without discomfort, and the casement, that uncloses to release the lingering smoky ghost of the last fire upon the hearth, lets in a sunny spirit whose only flames and sparks shall be roses and humming-birds!

In terms not unlike these did I express the sentiment of the season to Miss Agonies* Blatherly,— only filial expense of the Hon. Senator Blatherly, of Pequog, as I escorted her some mornings ago to select her new spring things for the Impeachment. It was "Opening-day,"— that day of deep thought, and much milliner's bill, when the subtle mind of woman devises its most touching appeals to the funds of the thing called Man,— and while the carriage rolled slowly along the Avenue I spoke as I have written.

---

* Agonies is the fashionable pronunciation of Agnes.

"Oh, spring is perfectly sweet," she responded, with thoughtful earnestness; "and pa says that the spring-lamb will be heavenly this year; but some of the mantilla-jackets they're wearing now are utterly horrid."

"Still," said I, with great depth of feeling, "your sensitive woman's heart can scarcely take its usual delight even in the most expensive organdy, when you remember that the present spring is to witness the most solemn State Trial within the memory of man."

She met my penetrating gaze with a look of timid sympathy, and answered, with a sigh, —

"I shall wear a black French grenadine, with the back widths full and the front gored."

The remark indicated such an appreciative sense of the grave perils of the hour, that I could only press softly the little hand nearest my own, and tell her that her selection of black instead of gay colors, to wear to the Impeachment, would teach the world that woman knows how to feel for the inexpressible woes of her distracted country. I told her also, in trembling accents, that it would be a rebuke to those who opposed female suffrage on the ground that her sex knew not how to judge great national events; and besought her not to let her exquisite sympathy with the suffering nation lead her into too plain a waist.

An air of patient sadness and resignation characterized the whole aspect of the grenadine maiden, and said she, —

"Pearl-colored poplin with vandyke flounces, and tan-colored gloves, may do for the gay when pleasure's throng is nigh; but at such a moment as this, I love my afflicted native land too well to wear anything but jet bead trimmings and a Marie Antoinette scarf."

Think of this, my boy, in your own home, when some thoughtful, loving face bends over your shoulder, and a low, sweet voice asks to be taken to the Impeachment. Think of it when, in a moment of brutal irritation, you would speak sharply to the gentle creature who wishes to lay down her organdy and poplin for her country — and is none the less earnest in such self-sacrifice because she thinks that Impeachment must be something like the opera.

While Impeachment is being prepared for the stage, I pass much of my time in fashionable grenadine society, studying the fair young women of the Republic in all their beautiful intellectual phases; and as no one of them has thus far encouraged me to write her alone, I do now beg leave, with the utmost courtesy, to address them all.

You need not be informed, young ladies, that a majority of those excellent and rather mature persons hitherto favoring you with counsel and criticism in print have adopted a didactic and grievous strain, somewhat suggestive of those terrors to the young known as spectacles. There is at all times about a pair of spectacles a certain oppressive glare of severe human knowledge, — not to say patriarchal malevolence, — which continually forces upon observing youth a sense of infantile shortcomings, and a vague consciousness of unparalleled crime. The concentrated glare of the spectacles of six clergymen with blue umbrellas, at a fashionable revival meeting, has been known to make a fair girl of thirty utterly embittered against herself and her frivolous younger sister for two weeks; and it is upon record that a lovely seminary scholar, who had received a note from a young man of limited salary, was induced, by the spectacles of a maiden aunt, to confess herself guilty of murder.

The kind of literature suggesting spectacles is apt to have a like crushing and enfeebling effect, — causing the young partaker either to experience a morose realization of the general inability of youth to surpass palpable idiocy in anything; or to indulge in those untimely slumbers which notoriously indicate a criminal indifference to the most momentous interests of the celebrated Human Family. It may, indeed, be truthfully said, that the relentless reiterative references to that same domestic circle, in this kind of literature, have had a tendency to gift the minds of the incorrigibly immature with an impression of a "Family" wearing spectacles of the most vindictive manufacture, and continually glaring righteous indignation at an innumerable host of youthful conspirators against its most sacred rights.

Let it be my object then, young ladies, to counsel you, kindly and courteously, through the medium of a style betraying what may be delicately mentioned as the disrobed eye, — basing my supposition of your needs upon your comprehensive aspect to the undraped optic; and tendering advice at no time savoring more of artificial vision than may possibly be involved in an occasional hint of the two little orphan goggles casually bestriding the nose of innocent and harmless manhood.

Long and thoughtful contemplation of your delightful sex through a piece of Smoked Glass — which I use to protect my eyes from over-dazzling — has impressed me with a firm belief in the unquestionable superiority of all young ladies to their parents; and I would especially bring to your attention the manifest propriety of discountenancing any familiarity from your mothers when in society. If obliged to go with your tiresome maternals to any social gathering, you may reclaim your freedom immediately upon entering the room by slipping abstractedly away in the direction of the piano, and from thenceforth being artlessly forgetful of all messages forwarded to you, and miraculously blind to all beckonings and elevations of fans. Sentimental dry-goods clerks have, before now, been greatly stricken at heart by such evidences of refined feminine spirit; and distinguished foreigners have more than once been tempted into offering their hands and hearts, by well-timed exhibitions of filial contempt, — quite forgetful, in the enthralling excitement of the moment, of the wives they already had in their own countries.

In fact, this question of the management of would-be familiar mothers is of vital importance to the dignity of your whole young ladyhood, and should have a large part of its treatment at home, where forward mothers are only too apt to presume upon accidental amiability. Guarding yourselves vigorously against the vulgarizing entertainment of any old-fashioned idea of humdrum "duty," as the bores call it, let it be your business to watch jealously for the first approach to undue freedom on the part of the vain old ladies, and then give them immediately to understand that you are not children now, ma, if you please. This wholesome reminder, administered with a proper sweep of the skirts and pensive glance toward the nearest mirror, is one of the finest possible illustrations of firmness of character. Well-disciplined mothers will seldom venture to express unasked opinions regarding the colors and styles of dresses patronized by their daughters; but in cases where some momentary indulgence has deluded them into this greater liberty, there is nothing like a well-slammed door, or an immediate practice of the scales at the piano. Well-slammed doors and those eternal scales are the tremendous instruments of rebuke and torture with which your sex can at any time make life a burden to a whole flock of enemies.

In the subjection of your fathers to their proper condition of helpless neutrality and financial liberality, you must exercise more gradual measures; for a certain low kind of conceited importance clings to a man as long as he lives, and often incites him to desperate efforts for the enslavement of his natural owners — his children. It will be a great aid to your work of "reconstruction," if these necessary afflictions have the habit of smoking. You will then have a perfectly just excuse for seeing as little of them as possible, and gradually breaking their spirits and humbling them in their own estimations, by casually throwing out hints at the breakfast-table about being almost choked whenever you go near pa's room. Pa thus has impressed upon him a sense of his own degradation, and will feel himself but poorly compensating for the great trial he is to you, by abjectly and promptly responding to all demands upon his purse. He will also hand your fan and shawl to you after the ball, when some promising young man is to be emphatically recalled to a sense of his continued insignificance. In fact, a well-behaved father is useful in many ways, when trained with a firm hand, and the skill employed in teaching him his tricks is never wasted.

In regard to the piano which you all indubitably owe to society, young ladies, I would unhesitatingly counsel systematic violence in the whole Italian department, and a principled unconsciousness of the existence of any genteel compositions in English. That is to say, you should thus exhibit your piano in society; though at home it will be good policy to select some one national air as a means of embittering the souls of your parents against music forever, and thus ridding yourselves of those importunings for specimens of your skill with which only perfect strangers have any right to assail you. A really great effect can be achieved in company by miss-keying a little when you first take seat at the instrument, and then looking artlessly up at the most eligible set of whiskers present, as who should say: Oh dear! what a frightful creature I am! Promptly follow this by an impatient straightening-up, — an archly affectionate glance, as for playful help, toward some other young lady whom you have met that evening for the first time, — and an instant plunge of all your fingers into the most deafening of the notes; and you will make the eligible whiskers ruin himself with bouquets for you in less than a month.

Additionally to the piano, you also owe to society a strict abstinence from anything approximating to Nature; which, as all well-bred people know, is something vulgarly cheap and only patronized by the lower classes. You must select models for yourselves from those practitioners of the graces in your own sex whose fashionable campaigns have made them your superiors in art, and whom you will speedily know by the intense envy and hatred you will feel toward them from the first. The envy and hatred in question will not be what common people call by those names at all; they will really be the refined mental components of a high order of intellectual energy, developing in you a genius for imitation conserving the loftiest art.

To make perfect your Artificiality, however, — to make it irresistibly eloquent of womanhood's most exquisite sensibilities, — you must manage to subdue it here and there with little touches of girlish prettiness. Thus, when conversing in society, or even in the conservatory at home, with some eligible son of a rich Contractor, you can appear sweetly thoughtful and girlishly innocent by a judicious bit of by-play with your lace pocket-handkerchief. Supposing you to have prepared yourself beforehand with a handkerchief carelessly thrown over your shoulders, you talk yourself apparently into a gentle sort of dreamy abstraction; and then, with your eyes softly fixed on vacancy, though still talking, you unconsciously as it were carry one end of your handkerchief to the mouth with the forefinger of your right hand, and keep pushing it thus, inch by inch, through your lips as you stand, until the other end falls from your shoulders and the whole handkerchief drops to the floor. This rouses you from your pretty reverie with a start, and (if possible of production) a blush; you make a half-motion to pick it up; the eligible captive is too quick for you, however, and succeeds in lifting the prize just as the most enthralling of little slippers is darted out to save it. Don't you see the inimitable hit thus made? Don't you see how natural it must be after that for the eligible son of a Contractor to insist upon keeping the handkerchief, and thus hopelessly commit himself?

These little touches of girlish prettiness are indeed of the utmost importance to you, young ladies, and always convince the sensible masculine observer that you have those tender and confiding qualities of heart which would enable loving husbands to lead you by a thread.

I would even specialize one more of these touches, lest you in your uncalculating guilelessness should forget it. I would have you bear in mind the really beautiful device of having particular female friends of your own age, and rather plainer than yourselves, whose waists you can frequently embrace in public, and whom you can habitually salute as "darling love," "my precious," "*cheri*," or "my darling dear," when gentlemen are present. No eligible single gentleman was ever known to be proof against this Arcadian little — *will* you excuse me? — dodge. It is not *in* a single gentleman of means to make head against such an artless evidence of your inexpressible capacity for loving.

In the matter of conversation, society expects you to express ignorance of every material thing in the world as grammatically as possible. It also expects you to practise the phrase, "How Perfectly Ridiculous," until you can use it as a reply and comment to and upon everything not supposed to be of daily occurrence in high life. As, —

"Did you hear, Miss Gusherby, that your father's old partner had committed suicide?"

"How Perfectly Ridiculous!"

"O Morianna Gusherby! I shall never get over it — I'm sure I shan't. I saw a man run over in front of Stewart's to-day, and the stage-wheels went right over his face!"

"How Perfectly Ridiculous!"

Politics, of course, are too horrid to be talked about at all, save in that general easy and graceful superciliousness of tone toward anything original with your own country which infallibly indicates aristocratic elevation of sentiment. Quite a reputation for intellect, too, may possibly be gained by a rather scornful mention of Mr. Greeley as *un ami des noirs*. This is supposing, of course, that you have studied French sufficiently to know where to find convenient phrases in the back of Worcester's larger Dictionary.

Possibly you will accuse me, young ladies, of counselling you as though you were all expected to act precisely alike — were all to be exact repetitions, or reflections, of each other; but such implied and intolerable sarcasm is by no means characteristic of my courteous intent. In my large experience of the world and perfect familiarity with the most estimable qualities of your sex, I have seen the most brilliant effects produced, by some of you, upon plans quite distinct from those occupying so much of this letter.

For instance: I have known some of you to bless society with a real Sensation, by continually maintaining a Thoughtful and Sceptical aspect, — as though enduring the contact of the gay, giddy world only upon sufferance, and perpetually filled with a sadly-sweet longing for the spiritual companionship of barely one Real Friend. Your demeanor has conveyed an idea of the most touching, patient suffering, and you have allowed it to be whispered about that your life-long affliction is a want of True Sympathy, — an eternal yearning for Some One who can Truly Understand you. It is recorded, in some musty tradition or other, that this tone of bearing in the fashionable female young, was attributed by our rude ancestors to Dyspepsia, — a barbarous disease anciently produced by a too ardent addiction to boarding-school candies, vinegar, and slate-pencils. Now, however, all genteel persons know it to be an indication of a finely strung nature, and the young man who *can* Truly Understand does not struggle long against his fate.

To succeed in this plan, however, requires a force of character of which many fine feminine organisms are not at all times capable. Being aware of this fact, it affords me the greater pleasure to set, with all humility, before you, another and no less effective means of indicating distinctive traits to the world. It is possible for you to show a decided individuality by the Dressing of your Hair; and, perhaps, I cannot more clearly illustrate to you the wonderful use of Hair-dressing alone to epitomize all that there is of distinguishing character in your gracious sex, than by submitting to your indulgent attention an authenticated biography of

THE HAIRESS.

I.

In Rutgers' halls a maid I knew,
    With her hair unbecomingly dressed;
She'd lips of red and eyes of blue,
    With her hair unbecomingly dressed;
Such a taper waist and a lovely arm
And shoulders white were enough to charm

---

* Rutgers' Institute, a fashionable female seminary on Fifth Avenue, N.Y.

SMOKED GLASS.

The sourest saint and his heart alarm —
    With her hair unbecomingly dressed.

II.

She had a brow of Grecian mould,
    With her hair unbecomingly dressed;
The nose that Venus wore of old,
    With her hair unbecomingly dressed;
Her rosy mouth was a kiss divine,
Preserved, as 'twere, in a ruby wine,
Through which its sweets, to tempt, might shine —
    With her hair unbecomingly dressed.

III.

She sat upon the scholar's bench,
    With her hair unbecomingly dressed,
To study music, Greek, and French,
    With her hair unbecomingly dressed;
She flirted with Signor Shaykantrill,
Who taught her opera and quadrille,
And managed of novels to read her fill,
    With her hair unbecomingly dressed.

IV.

They took her from the boarding-school,
    With her hair unbecomingly dressed;
And had her robed in silk and tulle,
    With her hair unbecomingly dressed.
She entered society's bright pell-mell,
And took the palm of the reigning belle,
And cast upon every heart a spell,
    With her hair unbecomingly dressed.

V.

She drove a phaeton in the Park,
    With her hair unbecomingly dressed;

RAIL ENJOYMENT.

Came back to dinner just at dark,
  With her hair unbecomingly dressed.
She went to the matinée, ball, and rout,
To dance, to simper, to smile, and pout;
And then to the Springs when the ton went out,
  With her hair unbecomingly dressed.

VI.

Not long had such a nymph to wait,
  With her hair unbecomingly dressed;
For one to be her lord and mate,
  With her hair unbecomingly dressed.
'Twas the son of a heavy dry-goods man
One night at a hop picked up her fan;
And she promised to share his heart and span,
  With her hair unbecomingly dressed.

VII.

Returned to town an autumn-bride,
  With her hair unbecomingly dressed,
She took a coach, and ma inside,
  With her hair unbecomingly dressed;
Went straight to Stewart's to buy the things
That women wear in the place of wings,
And ordered of Tiffany pearls by strings,
  With her hair unbecomingly dressed.

VIII.

She had a wedding *à la mode*,
  With her hair unbecomingly dressed;
And then to Jersey Ferry rode,
  With her hair unbecomingly dressed;
For Washington City they took the train,
Where the honeymoon should wax and wane,
And over the rails she sped amain,
  With her hair unbecomingly dressed.

SMOKED GLASS.

IX.

The nation's wisdom greeted her,
    With her hair unbecomingly dressed;
She made the season all astir,
    With her hair unbecomingly dressed;
She flirted with Senators sharp and snub,
While her liege and lord was at the club,
And shone supreme at dance and rub,
    With her hair umbecomingly dressed.

X.

Her husband saw her doing thus,
    With her hair unbecomingly dressed;
She begged him not to make a fuss,
    With her hair unbecomingly dressed;
But he was resolved on a homeward trip,
And little he heeded her pouting lip,
And home she came in his bearish grip,
    With her hair unbecomingly dressed.

XI.

Upon the train she felt a chill,
    With her hair unbecomingly dressed;
It made her quickly very ill,
    With her hair unbecomingly dressed;
The bonnet she wore was so very small
That it scarcely seemed a bonnet at all;
And how could she cover her head in a shawl,
    With her hair unbecomingly dressed?

XII.

Arrived in town she went to bed,
    With her hair unbecomingly dressed,
And coughed enough to split her head,
    With her hair unbecomingly dressed:

> The doctors came in a stately host,
> And with powder and pill the patient dosed;
> But in less than a week she became a ghost,
>   With her hair unbecomingly dressed.

XIII.

> In garments rich she slept her last,
>   With her hair unbecomingly dressed;
> And to a better world had passed,
>   With her hair unbecomingly dressed;
> Where the snow melts first in the breath of spring,
> And the sweetest birds the latest sing,
> She waits the great awakening,
>   With her hair unbecomingly dressed!

And now, that I have humbly and modestly tendered all this earnest advice to you, let me add the wish that you may "Ever be happy," and thus qualify yourselves to become ultimately the "Pride of the pirate's heart." You have throngs of manly admirers always around you, many of whom are even ready to become husbands as soon as they can afford it; but not one of them all is more devoutly an adorer and slave, young ladies, than the retiring individual who counts it the sum of all earthly honors to sign himself

              Your own Chevalier,
                    ORPHEUS C. KERR.

LETTER IV.

EXPLAINING THE SURPRISING EQUANIMITY OF A NATION UNDER COMPLICATED MISFORTUNES BY THE PARALLEL CASE OF A GREAT PHILOSOPHER OF THE SIXTH WARD; CONFESSING THE INEXPLICABLE LEVITY PRODUCED BY THE HONEST SENTIMENTS OF A SOLID BOSTON MAN; AND CELEBRATING THE GRAND OPENING OF THE THEATRE OF WAR WITH THE SPECTACULAR DRAMA OF IMPEACHMENT.

WASHINGTON, D. C., March 26, 1868.

EVEN as the exciting able editor of some reliable American morning journal surveys the whole world from his third-story backroom, and is sufficiently weakened in his mind thereby to write such an article on the Present State of the Universe as shall at once fill out a column, and spare his subscribers the shock of being tempted to read the "editorial page" for once in their lives; so do I look abroad, my boy, from the window of my room at Willard's upon this entire humorous nation of ours, and am so enfeebled in intellect by the spectacle of its unspeakable equanimity under Reconstruction and Impeachment, that orders for thoughtful newspaper-articles upon the Progress of Democratic Principles in Russia may be forwarded at once to my address. As I look thus extensively abroad — after incidentally nodding in a chaste and pleasing manner to a grenadine maiden at another casement — I cannot help observing to myself, "This is, indeed, equanimity," and reminds me of what once occurred in the Sixth Ward.

In that cradle of American liberty in which many a one has been "rocked" by political persons of Irish descent, there formerly resided a middle-aged top, of dumpling forehead and continual fatness of smile, who went beaming around everywhere like a private sun with spectacles on, and passed through two panics, and a cholera season, with so much equanimity that his friends concluded he must be either a statue of George Washington or a great philosopher. Did a vast fire break out in his district, an election go this way or that way, or a riot destroy all his neighbors' windows, — this fine old top would be out next morning in a perfect sunrise of contented smile, covering everybody all over with placidity, and being taken by strangers for both Benjamin Franklin and Mr. Greeley. Did half his family try to put him out of the house, or his two only sons half kill each other in a domestic fight, — this calm old top would keep shining on harder than ever, and plastering up his head and going to his daily business with such bright looks that many mistook him for an unmarried man. Persons from other wards would go to him and expostulate against so much equanimity, — telling him that it injured the value of their property and produced sickness in their minds; but he only shook hands with them all round in an extremely affectionate manner, and went beaming away to attend the funeral of his brother.

At last, however, a crowning calamity seemed to threaten

this radiant top, and all his wife's relatives hoped that his time had come. In a high-moral life insurance company, of which he was an immense stockholder, a great dispute took place between the President and the Board of Directors. The former, between two meetings of the Board, took the responsibility of getting out a new style of "Policy," by which the person who insured under it was obliged to assert no more than that he had a sound Constitution. The Secretary of the Company, who had been made such under a former President, opposed this style of Policy with all his might; whereupon, the President suspended him from office, put in a Secretary *ad interim*, removed such agents of the Company in other cities as refused to adopt the new Policy, and commenced doing such a wholesale Constitutional business that all creation bade fair to be insured in a month. Then came the Meeting of the Directors, a majority of whom were patent-medicine men, and who, in the original Policy, had specified not only that the insured should have sound Constitutions, but that said soundness should have been specially produced by the use (affirmed under oath) of their patent-medicines. The Directors reinstated the original Secretary and Policy; the defiant President was arraigned before the Board with a view to his supersedure by the Vice-President; and, in the ensuing public scandal, the whole business of the Company stood still.*

---

* Substitute the word *Reconstruction* for "*Insurance*," and this is a just and exact illustration of the quarrel between President Johnson and Congress.

Then all the wife's relatives of the middle-aged and philosophical top believed that they had him at last, and repaired in a body to his private residence to witness the overwhelming defeat of his equanimity; but to their unspeakable disgust they found him perusing, in great comfort, the latest news of the trouble in a stentorian daily journal, the while his features shone with that debilitating serenity which eternally characterizes the photographs we have taken for our unmarried female friends.

"Old man!" cried the relatives, rending their garments, and feeling sorry for it immediately after; "do you realize that this quarrel will ruin you, by making your stock in the Company worthless? How, oh how! under this last awful go, can you exhibit so much equanimity?"

"My friends," said this vivacious top, with a pleased expression, "why should I shed the briny? Under the Director's 'Policy' there would never be any business at all, which would be ruin. Under the President's 'Policy' the business would be wholesale recklessness, which would be ruin; and in the fight between the two Policies there is ruin any way. Give my love to your families, and send in the Sheriff."

After which the imperturbable top went cheerfully humming to put on his gaiters; and tripped away, with the utmost satisfaction, to register his name under the Bankrupt Act.

I have been thinking, my boy, I have been thinking, that perhaps the curious medical treatment of having its lower limbs kept in hot water for years, accompanied by the amazing surgical operation of having its head slowly sawed off, may not be the surest means of restoring health to the nation; and that the inexpressible equanimity of the latter under Reconstruction and Impeachment may possibly be based upon a philosophy like that which I have celebrated.

Discussing this and other great questions, I was walking down Pennsylvania Avenue with a solid Boston man yesterday, when we ran against a fellow-being who, with his back toward us, was attentively contemplating our national banner as it floated over a building near by. With arms folded, head thrown back, and the south-east corner of the Ten-of-Clubs accidentally protruding below the lining of his soft black hat, he reminded me somewhat of Hamlet, just prior to his little affair with Laertes; but, upon looking more closely, I recognized the Conservative Kentucky Chap.

"Well met, my 'Knight of the Golden Circle!'" cried I, introducing my friend; "what cheer?"

"Hem!" says the Kentucky Chap, "the National Democratic Organization, of which Kentucky is the pride, knows nothing whatsoever about any golden circle except the 'Whiskey Ring.'"

Here the Conservative Kentucky Chap gazed again at the floating standard, and says he, —

"When I look upon that picture of Kentucky's starry sky, and remember that ten stars in the constellation are still kept in eclipse by the negro-suffrage despotism of New England, I feel as though the ten of diamonds had slipped out of the pack and left Kentucky to be euchred by New Hampshire."*

Here the solid Boston man breathed very hard, as though he had just arisen from his usual morning prayer to Dickens, and says he, —

"Did you speak to me, Rebel?"

The Kentucky Chap scowled such an intense frown of assent that the four of clubs worked down out of his hat to the brow of his left eye, and gave him the appearance of being under treatment for ophthalmia.

"That flag is for every American freeman!" says the solid Boston man, "and is favorably mentioned in the works of Dr. Holmes as such. Next to the Hoosac Tunnel and Ticknor & Fields' new bookshop, it is dearer to every loyal bosom, whether white or black, than all else in the wide world. And shall its stars shine for the white Rebel while the sable loyalist is forgotten? Forbid it, Bunker Hill! I tell you," exclaimed the solid Boston man, growing purple in the face, "that Massachusetts has at length decided to raise the free-negro race to their birthright under the national stars, even though it should be necessary to trust that flag entirely to black guards!"

He meant it honestly, my boy; he almost cried under his keen sense of the magnanimous intention of Massachusetts; but upon catching the intensely cocked eye of the Conservative Kentucky Chap, I coughed in a manner quite unfamiliar to our highest-priced physicians; and slapped

* New Hampshire had just elected a Republican State ticket.

Kentucky's favorite son so severely upon the back, to save him from inexplicable choking, that a small black case-bottle and three court-cards shot out of his forward vestments like meteors from a cloud.

Fain would this friendly pen pursue the theme, were it not for a card inscribed as follows, —

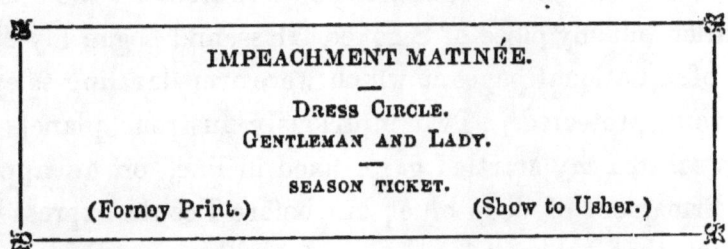

IMPEACHMENT MATINÉE.

Dress Circle.
Gentleman and Lady.

SEASON TICKET.

(Forney Print.)   (Show to Usher.)

This ticket lies here upon my desk; and below it is a smaller one, answering to the between-acts "check" of other theatres, and intended for use at the door when you desire to leave for a few moments. It is inscribed, simply,

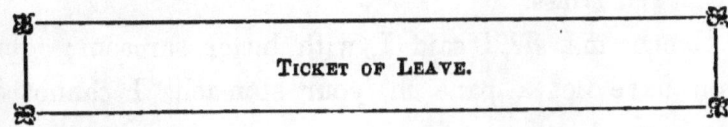

Ticket of Leave.

and admits the bearer to the theatre again, after he shall have procured the glass of water and eaten the clove, to lunch upon which he went out.

Promptly, at one o'clock, on two days of this week, I used the first of the above tickets, and had the pleasure of escorting a fashionable maiden, of imperceptible bonnet, to one of the best seats in the house. Let this agile pen move slowly, my boy; and this ink, which is of the color of the freed-negro race, flow gently, while I recall the scene that burst upon my vision and must have broken many pairs of spectacles. After seating the maiden, and giving her half an hour to complete that pulling of skirts with which the bell-shaped women of America are wont to soothe the nerves of all beholders at church and the opera, I pulled out my piece of Smoked Glass, and began my survey of a national pageant which were over-dazzling to eyes not thus protected. Two injuriously lustrous planets at once saluted my startled gaze, fixed in line, on an apparent firmament of deep blue; but before I could express the opinion that I must be going mad, or that something seriously astronomical must be the matter with my orbs, the shining twain resolved themselves into two gorgeous brass buttons upon the cerulean dress-coat of a military being who had affably taken a standing position right in front of my Smoked Glass.

"Excuse me, sir," said I, with bitter sarcasm; "but, as you have not a pane in your stomach, I cannot see through you."

"Ah!" said a familiar voice, "if I'd thought of that, my fren', I'd have worn my sash."

Directing my Smoked Glass to his face, which was now turned toward me, I recognized Captain Villiam Brown; who, with his own bit of glass, had been engagingly observing the innumerable organdy and grenadine maidens in the dress-circle.

"Ha, my Lord Cardigan," said I, after excusing myself to the lady in my own care, and moving away with the Mackerel hero, "do you come here to study the Black Crook which our national affairs seem to have taken, or are you present rather as an indifferent spectator of the White Forney?" *

"My fren'," says Villiam, taking a handful of peanuts from one of his pockets and giving me half, "I come to the High Court of Impeachment to examine the fashions, and see whether bonnets have got low enough yet to make it safe to enter into the 5-20 bonds of wedlock."

"I don't know about the bonnets," said I, calmly; "for my Smoked Glass does not magnify enough to reveal them to me. But this season's dresses are certainly low enough — in the neck."

"Ah!" says Villiam, severely; "the dresses of some of these fair beings are so low, that they are virtually a take-off of everything our mothers used to wear. Hum!" says Villiam, anxiously, "some of them will take cold in this changeable weather if they don't put on more fans."

Thus speaking, he left me, and I hastened to the grenadine of my choice, carrying thither one of the programmes, reading thus, —

---

* The "Black Crook" and the "White Fawn" were two spectacular ballets of the most meretricious "French school," which had, successively, occupied the stage of the metropolitan play-house for nearly two years, and rendered the latter eligible for the title of moral plague-house.

THEATRE OF WAR.

Managers and Proprietors, . . . Stevens & Co.
Treasurer, ... U. S. Bond.
Prompter, ... A. Whitehouse.

The management have the honor to announce the completion of their arrangements for the production of an entirely new adaptation from English and French theatres, entitled

IMPEACHMENT;
OR,
The Man Without a Friend;

which will be produced with the following great cast: —

Man Without a friend, ... A. Johnson.
Macbeth, ... B. Wade.
Mephistophiles, ... Thaddeus Stevens.
Iago, ... Manton Marble.
Mrs. Caudle, ... H. Greeley.
Harlequin, ... J. G. Bennett.
Joseph Surface, ... H. J. Raymond.
First Supernumerary, ... S. P. Chase.
Deserters, ... Democratic Party.
Corps de Bully, . . . Butler, Bingham, & Co.

To be followed by the ever-popular farce of
"RECONSTRUCTION,"
to which has recently been added an Alabama breakdown.*

Performance commences with an Overture (for "more time") . . . By Mr. Stanbery.

---

* By popular vote, unreconstructed Alabama had recently rejected the Constitution which would have restored her to representation in Congress.

As I looked down from the dress-circle into the pit during the opening scenes, and brought my bit of Smoked Glass to bear upon one after another of the great actors, there came upon me an unseemly disposition to mislead the intellect of the innocent being at my side, and encourage her to believe that the scene then "on" was intended to represent a fashionable dining-saloon.

"Why," she whispered, "does that fine-looking creature, at the top table, rap so?"

It was the Chief Justice rapping for order, but I told her that he was knocking for a waiter to come and take his order.

Was this wrong, my boy? Did I thereby cast ridicule upon the majestic judicial proceedings of the United States of America, and fill the subtle mind of woman with mistaken imaginings? Perhaps so, my Pythias; perhaps so; but she thought that first scene was laid in an eating-house, and kept wondering why the tables of the Counsel and Managers were not furnished at least with some representative of Ham.

Speaking of the latter, I was conversing last evening with the former chaplain of the Mackerel Brigade, concerning the President's line of defence; and suggested to him, that, inasmuch as Mr. Johnson is a tailor by profession, and therefore, according to popular belief, only one-ninth of a man, it was palpably unfair for the Senate to be his jury.

"How so?" asked the chaplain.

"Why," said I; "can there be any fairness in pitting a one-ninth-er against so many Se'n-a-tors?"

"Young man," quoth the Mackerel Chaplain, abstractedly; "the judgment of Heaven has fallen upon the President because of his recreancy to the hapless children of Ham, whose Moses he had promised to be. A black hand stretched to Deity in a prayer for merited retribution may be stronger than the white hand that invokes a blessing undeserved."

How true that is, my boy, especially when you remember of what little account has been that blessing once invoked for yourself by the hand of your father! A. Johnson is doomed. Off with his head! So much for bucking Ham!

Yours, Shakespeareanly,

ORPHEUS C. KERR.

LETTER V.

INTRODUCING AN IMPECUNIOUS BUT LOYAL SOUTHERN CAVALIER; DEPICTING A GORGEOUS STAGE-PROCESSION IN THE MIGHTY SPECTACLE OF IMPEACHMENT; REPORTING THE UNEXAMPLED AND CONVINCING INAUGURAL ARGUMENT OF MANAGER BUTLER, AND THE VISIBLE CONSTERNATION OF NERVOUS AUDITORS THEREAT.

WASHINGTON, D. C., April 3, 1868.

EVEN as the blue-and-brassy bee, with one knowing eye fixed all the time upon some goodly cabbage-rose, dallies with meaner flowers by way of adding relish to the sweet delayed, so do I aggravate myself with baser themes only to make the grander, when it comes, the full majesty of Impeachment. Be it known to you at last, however, that on the occasion of my second visit, with the Mackerel Chaplain, to the theatre where this successful piece is now running, we found at the entrance thereof one of the most loyal Southerners that ever refrained from taking up arms against the Union on account of sickness. His name is Loyola Munchausen, brother of Captain Munchausen, late of the well-known Southern Confederacy; and as I gazed upon his spring-overcoat neatly manufactured from four Confederate buttons and a bed-tick, his dress-hat composed of half a boot-leg, mounted on one of those rims of tin through which stove-pipes enter chimneys; his Parisian stock representing a spare strap with buckle from an old trunk, and his April waistcoat worked up from a remnant of once valuable stair-carpet, — I could not help murmuring sadly to myself, "He does not look as wealthy as he did."

At the moment of our meeting, this reduced but impressive Southern being was fumbling in the eastern pocket of a pair of nether-garments, which seemed to have been hastily made from a quilted green merino petticoat, and drew forth from thence the clam-shell which served him as a pocket-book. To spare his feelings, I dropped my glance to his feet, which were plainly encased in a pair of stirrups; but was not quick enough to avoid discovering that the sole contents of his treasury were a shoe-string, a burnt match, and a cancelled postage-stamp. Noticing my look, he loftily donned a pair of white cotton socks, in place of gloves, and says he, —

"What would you, Vandal?"

Grasping his left hand, and nearly wringing the sock off, I saluted him as the brother of the very mirror of chivalry, and reminded him that I had been a war-correspondent of an excellent Union journal while Captain Munchausen was a Confederacy.

"War-correspondent," says he, twirling the curtain-rod which he carried as a cane, "war-correspondent?" He smiled darkly; and says he, "In that case, the sunny South forgives you; for you must have been a real misfortune to her foes. I was about to purchase a ticket here, but find that I must have left that hundred-dollar bill in my other coat-pocket."

"Come in with us," said I, gravely, "for we have season-tickets for two; and, as the audience is almost wholly feminine, we should be at least three-strong to divide its staring and bad manners."

"The ladies, sir," observed Loyola Munchausen, kissing his right sock, "may stare at me in a manner which I would not tolerate in a man; for, as a true Southern gentleman, I adore the sex; but, sir, if one solitary Yankee Vandal presumes to fix upon me the gaze of a conqueror, there will be — ha! ha! — there will be another war."

After which he tucked the curtain-rod under one arm in a stylish and Malacca manner, settled the boot-leg and tin rim more firmly upon his brow, and accompanied us into the gallery, like one who had gone through a financial panic without detraction from his largest-sized demeanor.

Shall I confide unto you, my boy, how I lent the wealthy Southron my piece of Smoked Glass, through which to observe, without detriment to his sight, the most brilliant scene in our distracted national history; and pointed out to him all the great men I could think of, without troubling myself much as to whether they really were those great men or not? Shall I confide to you that I gave all the principal female names in history to as many spring-bonnets as I could see? Let me do nothing of the kind; for is not such conduct the exclusive privilege of the fashionable Washington correspondents of all our reliable morning journals?

But what is this procession that mine eyes behold, entering upon the stage?

THE SERGEANT-AT-ARMS,

proclaiming that Impeachment is now about to begin. Followed by

THE CHIEF JUSTICE,

asking himself the great question, "Am I am I, or am I not am I?"

After whom came

A BLACKSMITH,

to "rivet the attention of the audience;"

A CARPENTER,

to erect scaffolds for those disposed to "hang upon the speaker's words;"

A GARDENER,

to attend such as may be "withered by his invective;"

MAN WITH HOSE,

to extinguish parties "fired by his eloquence."

Succeeded by the following

MANAGERS:

Thaddeus Stevens,	Thaddeus Butler,
Thaddeus Bingham,	Thaddeus Logan,
Thaddeus Boutwell,	Thaddeus Williams,

Thaddeus Wilson.

COUNSEL:

Andrew Stanbery,   Andrew Curtis,
Andrew Evarts,   Andrew Nelson,
Andrew Grocsbeck,
Senators, Witnesses, etc.

This procession having come fully into view, Thaddeus Butler stepped forth to deliver the prologue of the piece, which he gave in the form of an

ARGUMENT.

"MR. PRESIDENT AND GENTLEMEN OF THE SENATE:— The onerous duty has fallen to my fortune to present to you, imperfectly as I must, the several absences of fact and law by virtue of which the House of Representatives will endeavor to sustain the cause of the people against the President of the United States, now pending at your bar. The difficulty of defining said 'people,' the unprecedented novelty of said 'cause,' the perfect gravity with which we are trying to do it all, and the evident propriety of holding out some idea that the questions to be submitted to your adjudication have just occurred to us,— each and all must be my excuse for giving you as much speech as human patience can endure.

"Now, for the first time in the history of the world, has a nation brought its Chief Magistrate to grief, by high legal process, for administering the powers and duties of his high office in a manner somewhat disagreeable to the feelings of those who expressly desired him to do otherwise. In other times and lands it has been found that despotism of this kind could never be brought to trial in the courts, save upon rejoinder of the defendant to recover costs and damages for frivolous prosecution, and, in the absence of assassination, constitutional nations were obliged to endure rulers who had been pronounced mad or imbecile by many whom those rulers had blindly neglected to appoint to high and remunerative office. Only recently, one of the most civilized countries in the world, and the one which we imitate and abuse the most, was obliged to submit for years to the rule of a king currently believed to be insane by every great man whom he had ever failed to make a prime-minister; and all this because nobody could hit upon any particular reason for his removal.

"Our fathers were wiser in founding our government, and provided, constitutionally, that a President 'shall' be removed, on conviction of 'treason, bribery, or other high crimes and misdemeanors.' The provision is exact and comprehensive in every particular, save one. It covers the whole ground of Impeachment, save the specification of just what a disagreeable man can be impeached for. This was wisely done, because human foresight must have been inadequate, and the most ingenious human intelligence must have failed in the task of anticipating anything like the fine point to which modern intellect has brought the art of impeaching.

"It may not be unamusing to remember, that the framers of our Constitution had their minds improved, and their pride of human calculation humbled, while at their noble work, by an exemplary case. In the previous year, only, Thaddeus Burke, from his place in the House of Commons of England, had impeached Thaddeus Hastings for the misdemeanor of governing India in such a manner as to absolutely render soldiers and politicians unnecessary there. The mails were continually bringing the gorgeous and burning speeches of the impeachers across the Atlantic; and the great stress laid in these upon the above facts, and upon the additional unheard-of enormity of Hastings not having made a fortune by his government, so worked upon the intellects of our fathers, that they at once gave up all earthly hope of anticipating what a man might be impeached for next, and left the document open for modern improvements.

"Now, therefore, we have the question; what are modern impeachable offences? To quote from the learned judiciary labors of my able friend, the Honorable Thaddeus Lawrence, of Ohio, we define an impeachable high crime and misdemeanor to be *an act committed or omitted in violation of the Constitution, or in obedience thereto; and this may exist without violation of any positive law or essential principle of government, yet be esteemed otherwise by those who, from any motive or purpose, desire to impeach.*

"The first criticism which will strike the mind on a thoughtful examination of this definition is, that some of the despotic outrages enumerated in it are not within the common-sense definition of Crimes. You will find, however, upon turning to certain notes on the commentaries of Thaddeus Blackstone, that '*when the words "high crimes and misdemeanors" are used in Impeachment, such words have no real meaning whatever, but are used merely to give unspeakable solemnity to the charge.*' It being settled, therefore, that Impeachment may ensue from an act either committed or omitted, and that the terms of the accusation have really no earthly meaning, we next proceed to consider whether there actually exists any tribunal to try the case.

"The important question is, 'Does this Senate now sit as a Court, a Jury, or a Coroner's Inquest?' . The Constitution seems to have determined it to be the latter, because, under its provision, a man must be politically deceased before he can get any justice from it. You cannot be a Court, because there is no sign of law about any of your proceedings. You cannot be a Jury, because you cannot be challenged, and have made up your minds before hearing a word of the case. You consult no laws except the laws of health, and hold an Inquest by those rules only which refer to Parliamentary 'bodies.' You are a law unto yourselves and to no one else.

"In the first eight Articles of our charge the respondent is accused of removing Secretary Stanton, and appointing Mr. Thomas Secretary *ad interim*, when the latter was really of an opposite political party from ours; which brings before the American Senate and people this plain issue: Has the President, under the Constitution, the more than kingly prerogative to remove executive officers of his own appointment, and replace them by others who are not of our appointment? If the respondent can prove the affirmative, why then the great question arises, whether the Presidential office itself (if it has any rights whatever) ought, in fact, to exist as a part of the Constitutional government of a free people? If not, the respondent has no business to be President at all; and whoever votes 'not guilty' on our Articles, votes to subject our free institutions for four years to the presidency of any man who, being elected President, may choose to officiate as such.

"Article ninth charges that Major-General Thaddeus Emory being in command of the Military Department of Washington, respondent did feloniously express to him the belief that the Act of March 2, 1867, which provides that all orders from the President shall first be composed and afterward issued by General Thaddeus Grant, was inconsistent with any presidential existence at all, with intent thereby to induce Emory to feel some respect for him, and not treat Thaddeus Stanton better than himself. If this transaction stood alone, we might well admit that doubts might arise as to whether the respondent could be executed therefor; but when we find him subsequently offering a brevet to Lieutenant-General Sherman, is it not plain that he wanted to ingratiate himself with the army, so that at least one General would recognize him in the street? Is it not a high misdemeanor for the President to accomplish an act, which, in the opinion of Congress, if followed by another and different act, might lead to something more than has occurred?

"Article ten alleges that, intending to produce a question of the undoubted superiority of Congress in the odorous personalities of eloquence, he, Andrew Johnson, President of the United States, did make public speeches which, upon being compared with innumerable similar speeches by Congress from time immemorial, are calculated to produce the impression that Congress has at least a competitor in the art of political vituperation, and to destroy that confidence in the superior vulgarity of Congressional oratory which is one of the elements of our national complacency. Competition of this kind with the legislature has generally preceded a seizure by a despot of the legislative power of the country; and if we, through having set the example, cannot accuse the respondent of crime in attempting the first, we can at least assume for his destruction that he really must have intended the latter.

"The House of Representatives has done its duty. We have presented the absence of facts in a constitutional manner, and demand judgment at your hands, in preference to expecting it from your heads. I speak, therefore, not the language of exaggeration, but the words of truth and soberness, when I say, that the future political welfare of quite a number of persons, not accustomed to doing any thing for a living, hangs trembling on the decision of the hour." *

At the conclusion of this able argument, all of which I heard through my piece of Smoked Glass, quite a number of the audience who were not asleep fled stealthily from the house with a strange kind of terror in their faces.

"Why is this?" ejaculated I.

"They fly," says the Mackerel Chaplain, solemnly, "because they know not at what hour they, too, may be impeached. It is a serious time we live in, and who can tell when he, she, or it, may be impeached?"

Put your house in order, my boy; for if you have either committed or omitted any act whatsoever, you are guilty of a very high crime and misdemeanor.

Yours, criminally,
Orpheus C. Kerr.

* See Appendix for the original of this great Argument, 1.

LETTER VI.

WHICH ATTEMPTS THE SUBLIME, BUT SUCCEEDS TO A CERTAIN EXTENT ONLY; YET QUOTES FAVORITE PASSAGES FROM THE PREVAILING DRAMA AS THEY ARE BEING SIMULTANEOUSLY GROUND OUT, TO GREAT APPLAUSE, BY "ORGANS" ALL ABOUT THE COUNTRY.

WASHINGTON, D. C., April 9, 1868.

Though crash linked thunders on the ears of all, like Titan statues crumbling in their fall; though burns the lightning over wires of rain, as gods to gods did telegraph the slain; though rocks Creation with the battle's din, and Heav'n's own portals let the war-fiends in; still, above all, slow circling in the sky, dark as the storm and as the azure high, sweeps the lone Bird whose wing-ed throne of air finds in the whirlwind but a higher stair. Still, while the tempest laps all earth below; still, while his eyrie reels to thunder-blow; still, while the clouds from night to instant morn blaze at his feet a nest for demons born, crown of the gale in steady ring he flies, scathless, of iron beak and glittering eyes; and the red bolts that rive a world in wrath fright not his pinions from their solemn path.

I allude, my boy, to that philosophical fowl, the American eagle, whose unspeakable equanimity under national disaster was what may be termed the egg of my lay two weeks ago, and to which I return with a still loftier lay on this occasion. It is a curious and bewildering thing to behold a bird of such unconquerable equilibrium, and I was exchanging notes upon the subject with Captain Samyule Sa-mith, when we were joined by a respectable chap, of much tight pants, from New York.

"Well, my Central Parker," said I, impressively, "how beats the pulse of the Empire State? Does the great case, now being tried, excite in you that serious interest and grave foreboding which every thoughtful patriot should feel?"

"It does! it does!" sighed he, hastily putting on his eye-glasses to look more like Fifth Avenue. "We all feel anxious — most anxious about the trial, since its result must affect millions. This is indeed a serious time, and woe be unto us if victory remains with the narrow-gauge men."

"Yes, indeed," says I, sorrowfully; "those men who presume to dictate everything to others by their own narrow gauge, think more of themselves than of their country." I shook his hand in deep sympathy, and says I, "And what will you do in that event?"

"Why," says he, "we shall still take stock in the wide-gauge; believing that it is sure, in any event, to reach Chicago."

"You believe, then," said I, appreciatively, "that a wider gauge of thought will be adopted by those who are shortly to meet in Chicago for the nomination of a new President?"

He looked at me severely, and says he, "Would you be kind enough, my inebriated friend, to tell me what you are talking about?"

"The Impeachment Trial," says I, sternly. "What other great case should I mean?"

"Oh," says he, "you spoke so seriously, that I thought you meant the Erie Railroad case. I don't know much about the other case."

"Samyule," said I, hotly, "what do you think of such a state of public sentiment as this?"

"Well, really," says Samyule, thoughtfully, "it appears to me — it really appears to me," says Samyule, "that I never saw so much equilibrium."

Bird of my Country! never mind what happens, but just keep soaring on. If a few earthquakes should happen to your native land at any time, accompanied by small-pox, a new poem by Mr. Tupper, and other great calamities, you will probably take that occasion to conduct yourself like a cheerful canary.

In this state of things, my boy, when the terrible and majestic drama of Impeachment fails to infect our American fellow-beings with that seemly gravity which such a performance should produce, it will not pay me — it positively will not pay me, my boy, to treat of it in my most expensive and dignified manner. Mr. Greeley's very longest "Advice to Young Men" was never received with more scandalous alternations of slumber and levity than an unworthy but comic nation has given to this impressive production; and I come of too respectable a family to set forth all the awful details of an inexpressible public solemnity merely for the benefit of an unseasonably hilarious populace. When a great and exciting people get down to this depth of irreverence, it is time for Bancroft, Motley, and myself to spare ourselves a little in the more sacred portions of our historical works.

Believing, however, that there may be here and there a reader who, from being married, or from having undertaken to read the last number of the "Atlantic Monthly," is sufficiently wretched in his mind to take an interest in the miseries of his country, I will quote for his benefit a few passages from the dialogue of the terrible drama now acting here, —

SCENE, — THE HIGH COURT OF IMPEACHMENT.

(The Senate discovered sitting as a Court. Enter Chief Justice, Managers of Impeachment, Counsel for President, and Witnesses.)

FIRST MANAGER.

Oh, say, did you see, as aforesaid, one night,
  The person now known as *ad interim* Thomas,
Whose broad straps and three stars on his shoulders upright,
  The paraphernalia of greatness were rum as?
Did his eyeball's red glare, and his bomb-bursting air,
Give proof that the President told him to scare
Our War-Office Stanton, and cause him to waive
His right to such place in the land of the brave?

FIRST WITNESS.

When last I saw old Thomas,
    'Twas at a fancy ball,
He had his regimentals on,
    And looked uncommon tall.
I asked him what he meant to do
    If Stanton urged a doubt
Concerning what he'd power to try?
    He said he'd kick him out.

CHORUS.

As we talked of the place of war
That man of the army star,
    Good-natured old soul,
    Would have told me the whole,
Had I let him progress so far.

COUNSEL FOR THE PRESIDENT.

Believe us if all those familiar remarks
    Thou hast heard from another were thine,
They would still be as dear to these manager-sharks,
    And meet a construction as fine.
But we here cannot see why the language should be
    As President Johnson's construed.
And herewith we protest, with our hand on our breast,
    Against all such evidence crude.

FIRST MANAGER.

We can prove conspiracy
    By the words he used, sir,
'Twixt the President and him —
    If we're not confused, sir.
Witness, tell us all you said;
    Likewise all the man did.
Tell the tale, and keep it up,
    And with the Court be candid.

FIRST WITNESS.

If you fail (said I to him),
   Try, try again.
Delaware expects you to
   Try, try again.
All that other folks can do,
Why, with patience, may not you?
Delaware expects you to
   Try, try again.

If I do (said he to me),
   Try, try again,
Minister of War to be,
   What happens then?
What if Congress catch me there?
You'll (said I) be still as fair
In the eyes of Delaware.
   Try, try again.

COUNSEL FOR PRESIDENT.

'Mid Delaware's apothegms though he may roam,
We still can see nothing that brings the charge home;
A charm from the skies may well hallow them there,
But, search through the world, they're not wanted elsewhere.
   Come! come! But–l–er, come!
We wish to hear something that brings the charge home.

FIRST MANAGER.

Witness second, take the stand, —
Please to raise your honest hand,
   And we'll swear you to assert but what is true.
As reporter you'll revamp
All that Johnson on his tramp
   Through the Western States was pleased to say and do.
Tramp, tramp, tramp, you went reporting;
   Cheer up mem'ry, now, and tell
What his speeches were about when the rabble called him out,
   And you caught his words of anger as they fell.

COUNSEL FOR PRESIDENT.

Witness discreet has lost his sheet,
And don't know where to find it; —

FIRST MANAGER.

Leave him to show't; he's many a note
That carries a tale behind it.

SECOND WITNESS.

The President's speech I remember right well —
Delivered in Cleveland, before an hotel;
His hearers were chaps in habiliments old,
Who had no large fortunes in silver and gold.
CHORUS. — "My countrymen," — Bully for Andy! — Shut up!
"Allow me to" — Traitor! — You Judas! — You pup!
How 'bout New Orleans! — "Just allow me to say,
Ri-tural, ri-tural, ri-tural, ri-day."

COUNSEL FOR PRESIDENT.

Though dear to your heart are the scenes of that wild-mood,
When fond recollection presents them to view,
Yet green as the meadow and simple as childhood
You take us to be, if you think that will do!
The cot of your father, the dairy-house nigh it,
You'd doubtless remember, and equally well;
But mem'ry's not evidence, — here we deny it, —
And dripping with "coolness" you must be to tell.

FIRST MANAGER.

We wish to prove respondent drunk
For a few days, a few days,
When he was trav'ling with his trunk,
A few days on his way.
He tried to speak all night,
He tried to speak all day;
His pace would tire a bob-tail horse,
And turn reporter gray.

COUNSEL FOR PRESIDENT.

If it won't be called a crime we must ask a little time,
Which, surely, you'll be lib'ral, in accordin';
Our witnesses at best are scatter'd East and West,
And some are on the other side of Jordan.

CHORUS OF MANAGERS AND SENATORS.

He has wounded the country that loved him,
   That cherished his image four years,
And we'll give you, his counsel, till Thursday,
   For sickness, for sorrow, and tears.
Like young birds escaped from the fowler
   You'll chance for the moment to feel;
But the snare has been set for the prowler,
   And you will be trapped by the steel.

CHORUS OF COUNSEL.

Oh, we will plead on Thursday, and Friday, and next day;
But we must not plead on Sunday, when Sabbath schools begin.
And we can plead on Monday, and Tuesday, and We'n'sday;
But we must not plead on Sunday for that would be a sin.

EXEUNT OMNES.*

It is some consolation for the friend of his country and of virtue to know, my boy, that much of this sacred music is popular enough to be ground by organs all about the country. Subscribe at once for some party "organ," if you disbelieve me, and the first week's experience of such melody shall make you regret the absence of that enlivening monkey which, when connected with the other organs, is not forever imprisoned in an editor's chair.

               Yours, organically,
                    ORPHEUS C. KERR.

* See Appendix, 2.

LETTER VII.

CHARGING THE RADICALS WITH THE CONTINUED AND EXASPERATING WET WEATHER; SETTING FORTH THE GREAT WRONG DONE TO THE CONSERVATIVE KENTUCKY CHAP; REPEATING A CONVERSATION IN THE BOXES AND SCENE ON THE STAGE OF THE THEATRE OF WAR; REMARKING THE FIRST OF THE SOLILOQUIES FOR THE DEFENCE; AND ANNOUNCING A VISIT FROM THE DIREFUL "KU-KLUX KLAN."

WASHINGTON, D. C., April 16, 1868.

WHEN matters have reached such a pass that an American citizen of Caucasian descent cannot even step out to get a glass of water and a clove for his cold, without carrying an umbrella along, it is time for every suffering member of our excellent national Democratic organization to ask himself, How long are we to endure this Radical rain of terror? Did we have as much rain as this in the days of Andrew Jackson, when the Constitution of our forefathers was respected, and an able Democratic organization drank so little water that storms were not needed to keep up the supply? Alas! my boy, the impeaching Jacobins now in power have plotted this wet season for the express purpose of making one Wade, and I firmly believe that the end will be dampnation!

'Twas on Tuesday morn that the Conservative Kentucky Chap undertook to preserve a slice of lemon from decomposition by wrapping it in four thingfuls of whiskey, one of sugar, and one of hot water; inclosing the whole in a fresh glass tumbler, and placing the preparation upon the window-ledge to cool until he should be able to add a spoon. Owing to the unseemly combination of the Radicals with the enemies of their country, a heavy shower at once came up, and so weakened the lemon that it became injurious to the constitution of Kentucky. Noticing the ghastly smile that overspread the Conservative countenance of the poor chap when he tasted the diluted fruit, and discovered how debilitated it had become, I touched his elbow, and says I, —

"Are the waters of disappointment bitter to the taste, my Knight of the Golden Circle? or do your features writhe thus because the fluid of Kentucky fails in its duty?"

The Conservative Kentucky Chap feverishly caught at an ivory faro-check, which had accidentally fallen from its place as one of his sleeve-buttons, and says he, —

"The favorite fluid of Kentucky will frequently fail in its duty, when that duty is two dollars a gallon; but that is not the cause of my suffering. Here have I been trying to make some lemon-syrup for my cough," says he, bitterly, "and it has been rained into until all the Old Rye is washed out. Hem!" says the Conservative Kentucky Chap, fiercely, "if Kentucky has much more of her lemon-syrup spoiled by any more soaking rain whatsoever, she will believe that her Radical foes intend a second deluge, and demand an Ark."

"You think, then," says I, soothingly, "that this wet Radical weather tends to anarchy; and demand an Ark, in consequence, wherein to seek some safe place on a Conservative Ararat."

"Hem!" says he, thoughtfully, "those who want a place on ary-rat can have it; but Kentucky would prefer a place in the Custom mouse."

Another shower happening to commence just then, he went away through it like a despondent Noah, leaving me to ponder his words, and pay my usual visit to the theatre of Impeachment.

In regard to this latter temple of the moral drama, I may here say to you, my boy, that the business is steadily declining; and there have been no really good houses this week. The stars engaged by the managers have, in some instances, been so careless about learning their parts; the corps de bully has executed its faux pas, at times, with so little grace; the merry-Andrew men have given their break-downs with so little spirit, — that the patrons of the histrionic art in this city begin to weary of the play. On the day of which I am now treating, however, the fact that Sergeant O'Pake, of the unconquerable Mackerel Brigade, was to make his first appearance, and that a great soliloquy was to be delivered, caused quite a fair audience to assemble.

Lovely woman was there, with just enough spring-bonnet on to constitute a private crosswalk on the elaborate Central Park of her head; and didn't rustle her dress much more than enough to drive seven middle-aged amateurs of Impeachment to distraction. But what shall I say concerning the conduct of those unmarried male beings, in yellow kids and disgracefully short skirts, who kept leaning over the seats, between the bonnets, like dislocated pairs of tongs between fancy feather-dusters, and audibly informing the latter just how the play was going to turn out?

"But tell me, De Mortimer," whispered one fair girl, "does the hero of the piece prove himself innocent of all the High Crimes, and marry Miss Demeanor at last?"

"No, Miss Smytherly," returned De Mortimer; "Thaddeus Butler, you know, who represents the heirs to the Jonathan estate, insists upon it that Jonathan himself has become so weakened in his Constitution by internal rupture, that it is better to cut off his head at once and divide his property. The hero, you see, objects to this, and pretends that Jonathan's Constitution may be saved yet, and refuses to be himself cut off from attending the invalid until the latter tells him to go. Very well, then, say the heirs, if that is your plea, we'll meet it by assuming that Jonathan is already dead. This court, say they, is actually sitting as a Coroner's Inquest, and must order Jonathan's head cut off in order to justify its own sitting, — else, why should it make Inquest? So all the Coroner's Jurors have to decide that way, you know, and find the hero guilty of trying to prevent the Inquest; and Mr. Wade is appointed administrator."

"How perfectly ridiculous!" says Miss Smytherly.

"Oh, yes," says De Mortimer; "but the piece is from the French, you know, and must be Frenchy. The corps de bully is the real attraction, you see, and the rest but a mere excuse for introducing it."

This style of whispering at a play may be all very well, my boy, for the fragile female mind, which can't bear suspense; but there may be persons in a theatrical audience who do not care to have the whole interest of the plot anticipated for them.

After which biting sarcasm at the expense of the male being in yellow kids, I proceed to note the début of Sergeant O'Pake, who, having recently taken the pledge, has refused to take a brevet with the President. Manager Thaddeus Butler looked at him obliquely, and says he, —

"Sergeant, you are now in the presence of your Maker and Myself to answer truly unto all that I ask you, and to refuse all answers to questions from the insects for the defence. At the time of your interview with the thing called Johnson, was he, or was he not, in such an attitude as to render it possible for him to offer you a brevet?"

O'PAKE. "He was."

MANAGER. "From the sound of his voice, was it likely that he could have asked you, audibly, to take a brevet with him, and thereby be bribed to become his ally in a usurpation?"

O'PAKE. "He was able to speak, and of course he

A very cross examination.

could have spoken audibly on any subject; but I am not prepared to —"

MANAGER. "I must insist on a direct answer to my question, without comment. Was the sound of his voice such that it would have been possible for him to ask you, audibly, — so that if another person had been present that person could have heard it, — to take a brevet with him?"

O'PAKE. "It was."

MANAGER. "That is sufficient. No sane member of the jury will dare to doubt, after this, that Johnson has attempted to corrupt the army. Have the maniacs for the defence anything to say to the Sergeant?"

ANDREW STANBERY, one of the counsel for the defence, tore his hair at this crisis, and says he, —

"You say, Sergeant, that our client was in such an attitude as to render it possible for him to offer you a brevet. Did he offer it?"

MANAGER BUTLER. "I object. The defendant is on trial for High Crimes and Misdemeanors, and his mere acts are of no account. What WE have to prove is that his attitudes rendered it possible for him to do what is charged against him."

CORONER (represented by supernumerary Chase). "The Court thinks that the last question is admissible, but will leave it to the Jury."

The Jury then took a vote, which resulted in forty-nine Thaddeuses against the question, to one Andrew for it.

Thereupon Andrew Evarts, another of the counsel, rent his garments with anguish, and says he, —

"Sergeant O'Pake, you say that our client's voice could have articulated a request for you to take a brevet with him. Did he request you to take it?"

MANAGER BUTLER. "I object. It is our purpose to prove that the prisoner's voice was such as to have made it possible for him to have articulated the request; and, presumptively therefrom, that he did do it. The own words of a criminal on trial are never accepted as evidence, and I am surprised that the learned insect on the other side has DARED to put such a question."

CORONER (represented by supernumerary Chase). "The Court is of the opinion that the counsel's question should be allowed, if that of the manager is, but will leave it to the Jury."

The Jury then took a vote, which resulted in forty-nine Thaddeuses against allowing the question, and one Andrew for it.

MANAGER BUTLER. "Sergeant O'Pake may withdraw. We have succeeded in proving by him that the criminal is presumptively guilty, by being in an attitude, and having articulate ability, to intoxicate and corrupt the army with brevets.* The managers will now go to their dinners, and advise the Jury to do the same, while the learned Andrew Curtis delivers his soliloquy for the defence."

* General Sherman's testimony.

Two days, my boy, were occupied by this soliloquy, during which the jurors ate sandwiches, wrote home to their families, and animatedly discussed the prospects for the Presidency in 1868. It was really a great courtesy to the counsel for the defence to allow their associate the use of the Senate Chamber for the delivery of his soliloquy; and the delicacy with which the whole Court refrained from listening to a single word of it must have afforded him and his associates all the luxury of being entirely alone; yet Andrew Stanbery has been sick ever since.

At a late hour last evening, as I sat reflecting upon all this in my room at Willard's, a member of the freed-negro race brought me a card inscribed thus, — *

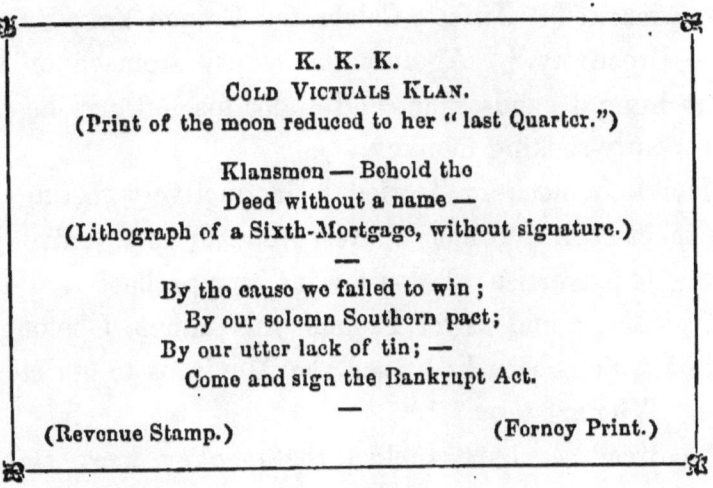

* Appendix, 3.

As I perused this mystic and awful document, the perspiration came out freely upon my lofty brow, and I turned to the member of the freed-negro race in trembling haste.

"Who gave you this?" asked I, fearfully.

The honest African's teeth chattered, and says he, — "S'help me gad, I don't know, mars'r; but I think he's a gemman from de Alms House."

"Show him up," said I, with great agitation.

The freed bondman disappeared, and in four moments thereafter I beheld a dreadful figure entering my room. It was a tall, gaunt shape, wearing an overcoat striped blue and red, and inscribed "Smithby's Patent Weather-Proof Awning." Over its shoulders, and hanging just below the waist, was an additional flowing white linen surtout, marked, "Jinks's Celebrated French Yoke Shirts. No. — Broadway." Against the empty stomach of the spectre hung a hand-organ, and under his left arm he carried a penny-seeking monkey.

"Horrible mockery," cried I, instinctively feeling for my pocket-book, "what wantest thou of me? I've got nothing to advertise; I don't want to purchase a waterproof awning; and as for French yoke shirts, I belong to a nation which recently helped the Mexicans to get rid of them. Who art thou?"

The dreadful shape tucked the monkey more tightly under his arm, and says he, —

"I'm the Ku-Klux Klan!" Here the spectre smiled

horribly, and deposited the half of a boot-leg which served him for a hat upon a table near my open window.

"Look out," says I, cautiously, "or that chapeau will blow into the street."

"It can't," says he, in a hollow voice; "there's a heavy mortgage on it."

Struck by the familiarity of the voice, I looked more closely at him, and recognized Loyola Munchausen. There he stood, a perfect walking-advertisement of the sunny South, and I paused to hear him speak again.

"My mission," says he, proudly, "is, in the first place, to ask if you have anything to advertise with my Klan, which is now issuing cards in every style, — 'K. K. K., — mortgages for all, — sign of a coffin. Try Jobbins's cough-drops, — sign of a dagger. Our Plantation Bitters are the Best, — sign of a serpent. Use Podger's Hair-Dye.' If you refuse to avail yourself of this popular medium, we fall back upon our countless wrongs, and demand — DEMAND, by Heaven! — that some quarter shall be shown the South."

I silently handed him a quarter.

"Do you want a tune for this?" says he, loftily, placing the money in his clam-shell pocket-book, "do you wish to witness the gyrations of the monkey in return for showing quarter to my section?"

Sadly I answered in the negative, and he departed as abruptly as he had arrived.

The South, my boy, may have slept once upon soft

down, but she is now hard up; and from what I have seen of the spring styles worn by her sons this year, I am firmly convinced that she sadly needs re-dress.

     Yours, charitably,
         Orpheus C. Kerr.

LETTER VIII.

CHANTING AN ASTONISHING LAY IN HONOR OF CLEAR WEATHER ONCE MORE; IRREVERENTLY LIKENING THE STATELY ABODE OF CONGRESS TO A STOMACH; MENTIONING AN ATTEMPTED SPECULATION WITH CAPTAIN SAMYULE SA-MITH, IN REAL ESTATE, AT TAIKACHOR COURT HOUSE; AND SAMPLING ANDREW NELSON'S SOLILOQUY.

WASHINGTON, D. C., April 25, 1868.

BEHOLD me emerging at last, my boy, from under an umbrella, and rejoicing to find the daily "Sun" issued once more in clear type, and exchanging only with the "Evening Star." To be sure, the recent rain came down in sheets and must have caused quite a rush to reed along the shore; but in our inland places like this we prefer to find the sun on our doorstep of a morning, and as the season advances, it will be more and more red. Surveying it with a speculative American orb of vision, I cannot but regret that it excludes all advertisements weather fair or foul; for who can doubt that, with its rising circulation in the East, and its "set" value in the West, it would be an invaluable medium for dealers in Light literature? But, after all, it rayses its terms too high for such use; and the gravity of our relations with it need not be disturbed by speculations as to how it can support itself while being furnished so cheaply to all creation as a "cent"-re piece!

I cannot explain just why I have taken such a printer's

view of old Sol at this season, unless it is because this season is called "printemps" in French; but I know that these two or three shiny days, after so much wet weather, have at once given me strong hopes of losing the moat from my own eye, and left me disposed for anything rather than the removal of the beam from my brother's eye. I am not a married man; I have no wife of my bosom to bear me little Bills, followed, mayhap, by a little Sue; and it is only natural that I should show some enthusiasm for the only sun I have. If not offspring, it is at least of Spring; and if I am not its father, it certainly cannot get much farther away from me. If not a parent in the ordinary sense to any particular son, this sun makes me apparent to all men, and that, too, without necessitating a mother-in-law, or putting me in peril of the fate of Othello, who, as everybody knows, was finally ruined by his wife's-smother!

And now, before it rains again, let me catch one more glimpse of the stately Capitol in this rare radiance; let my admiring glance rest yet another moment upon that swelling dome, which, like some impressive stomach in profile, with a figure of Liberty resting upon it as a fob watch-seal, catches the tawny lustre of the hour in massive repose. Smile, kindly skies, in lucent glory smile upon that abdomen of our distracted country, nor be tempted to administer any more of thy drops just yet, even though it has several panes across it. Make the watch-seal to glitter as though it really were something diviner than an ornament, and make the stomach to shine as though it were a luminous miracle of good digestion; and we will strive to believe for the moment that political choler might be one degree worse if it were cholera. Alas! how often do the wisest of us — we who pride ourselves, perchance, upon being the very Congressmen of private life — attribute certain ailings to our aching heads alone, or our lungs alone, or even to our hearts alone, while, all the time, it is actually the stomach that is deranged. The latter takes great satisfaction in appearing to be immaculate, and is always ready to bring about the impeachment of the head for causing headache, or to induce the reconstruction of the lungs, or heart, for imperfect circulation. Don't trouble yourself at all about Me, says the stomach, — I'm taking perfect care of my part of your Constitution; but you'd better impeach your head for aching, or the other part will be ruined. So, you impeach your head, and reconstruct your lungs; and, after all, it is solely the stomach that is at fault. Smile then, O kindly skies, in lucent glory smile upon the dome of yonder Capitol, and let there be clouds for the aching Head of the nation alone.

Thus apostrophized I, in thoughtful soliloquy, as I threw a last look toward the mighty theatre of Impeachment, before getting into one of the cars of the Grand Southern Trunk Railroad, the other day, to go with Captain Samyule Sa-mith to Taikachor Court House, Virginia. Samyule was attracted thither by a report that Pendragon Penruthers, Esq., a celebrated haughty Southerner of that place, had some fine old real estate to sell at great reduction, and I went with him to call a doctor at the places where the train should catch fire or roll down a bank.

The Grand Southern Trunk Railroad is so called because its cars are shaped like those fashionable travelling-trunks which can be thrown out of a third-story window without much breakage below the top and sides, by careful expressmen. When first built, just before the war, it was quite a good road to send your mother-in-law and poor relations over, and its trains seldom ran over a cow when they could get around her by going off the track. During the struggle with our excited national troops, however, the wealth of this great highway was seriously diminished; its daily receipts fell from four dollars to three and fourpence, and the large teakettle used in drawing trains was seized by our vandals to boil their coffee on several sanguinary occasions. Consequently, this famous through-route is now out of repair at some points of the line; and, until the President of the company can make enough money by his present occupation of apple-peddling to purchase a hammer and a few nails, the track will not be entirely safe for a high rate of speed.

Samyule and I wore padded India-rubber suits and fur caps to preserve ourselves from contusions at the stopping-places, and also kept our wills conspicuously pinned upon the breasts of our coats, in case we should go the wrong side of a bridge. Thus prepared, we calmly took our places upon the candle-boxes which served as seats in the first-class cars, and, as we went flying over the broomsticks which had been hastily laid down in place of the rails stolen by our vandals, our knives and watches were the only articles jerked from our pockets.

"Samyule," says I, holding fast to my candle-box, "don't it seem to you that this lightning-train sways a little in going around the corners?"

"You must be highly ineducated," says Samyule, instructively, "or you would know that this is a wide-gauge road, and can go as near to the rail-fences on either side as the engineer chooses."

Just then the locomotive sheered at something, and we struck a tree, which caused me to rise suddenly in the air from my candle-box, and come down upon the lap of a haughty planter, dressed in a rag-carpet surtout, who occupied an opposite seat. Having (as I learned afterward) received seven dollars and a quarter that day for his plantation from a Northern capitalist, this planter was unusually arrogant, and scowled upon me, as I sat on his knee, with dreadful malevolence.

"Sir," said he, grinding his teeth, "I do not wish to associate with one of your birth, and must request you to fly in some other direction when we have our next accident. I had an apple in my pocket for lunch, and you have crushed it."

"Do you think, then," said I, noticing that the next car was on fire, "that we shall live—"

But, at that moment, all the passengers shot from their candle-boxes toward the top of the vehicle, and we collectively began a series of swift aerial revolutions around the conductor and the stove. For our particular car had broken loose from the rest of the train by striking a telegraph-pole, and was turning over and over on its way to the nearest pile of stones. Luckily for Samyule and myself our fur caps and padded suits saved us from the usual fate of American railroad-excursionists, and, after picking ourselves out from the remains of the planters, we walked hastily from the ruins to a house near by.

This building, like the finer Southern mansions generally, had large white pillars on the front, and a heavy mortgage on the rest; and, when we rang the bell, it was answered by a tall, proud-looking man, who wore white kid gloves, a green gingham overcoat, and a pair of flannel drawers altered into pantaloons.

Samyule touched his cap, and says he, —

"Can you tell us, my worthy Count D'Orsay, how far we are from *Taikachor* Court House, and the residence of Pendragon Penruthers, Esquire?"

Perceiving that he was a Northern man by his good clothes, the embarrassed Virginian made a pass at him with an axe-handle which had been standing behind the door, and says he, —

"This place is *Taikachor* Court House, and I am Pendragon Penruthers, Esquire."

"Why, really," says Samyule, smiling agreeably, and drawing a pistol, "if that is the case, we have been expelled from the train at the right spot. Learning from all the reliable morning journals that the South now offers great inducements for the investments of capitalists, we have come down here to see how villages are selling. What could you say for this house?"

The Southerner brightened up, and says he, —

"Seven dollars and a quarter without the grounds; eight dollars with them." *

"And then," said Samyule, musingly, "I'd have to put two coats of paint on this villa."

"Two coats!" exclaimed Pendragon Penruthers, Esq. "One coat and a pair of pants would do."

"How so?" says Samyule, earnestly.

P. Penruthers smiled at his ignorance, and says he, —

"Why, you'd put the one coat on the house, and the pair of pants on the pillars."

"True," says Samyule, thankfully; "I should never have thought of that. Is that church yonder on your estate?"

"It is."

"How much for it?"

"Three dollars and a half."

"I'll take it," says Samyule. "Eight dollars and three and a half are eleven and a half. Here's the money."

The bargain being concluded, Mr. Penruthers invited us

---

* Fine real estate is really selling at absurdly low rates in some parts of the South, and persons of limited capital, who are willing to be shot or starved to death for the sake of having homes of their own, should hasten down.

into the fine private residence, where we were presently dining with him upon an inexpensive Indian pudding, wherein bits of alpaca were made to do duty for raisins, and a fruity claret wine, manufactured from boiled corks and coffin shavings, was served. At the termination of this sumptuous meal, the still arrogant Virginian notified us that he should retire to the hen-house until ready to depart for some other place, as he could not endure any noticeable length of existence under the same roof with those who, in military attire, had so recently ravaged the sunny South. Thus were Samyule and myself left alone in the purchased villa, and, after noticing that much of the furniture was in the style of Louis Quatorze,—supposing Louis Quatorze to have been much affected at that time by a taste for chairs with three legs,—we proceeded to calculate what income the estate was likely to produce toward paying its taxes. Looking forth upon the arable lands which he had purchased, through a bow-window which must have had a few whole panes of glass in it at some time during the previous century, Samyule estimated his coming grain-crop at about one straw-bed an acre; although one fine piece of meadow was so richly dressed with necks of bottles, old shoes, and discarded hoop-skirts, that it gave great promise as a fashionable building-lot for a junk-shop. At the conclusion of this survey, I volunteered to seek a grocery-store not far off and obtain something for supper; but when I got there, the Southern merchant in charge (attired in a coffee-bag) haughtily refused to sell anything to those who came to profit by the necessities of the sunny South, and I was obliged to return empty-handed. Furthermore, upon regaining the villa, I found that Captain Samyule Sa-mith had been waited upon in my absence by four members of the Ku-Klux Klan for cold victuals and small change; by a strong delegation of the freed-negro race for six dollars and a quarter, to start a Constitutional Convention; and that Pendragon Penruthers, Esq., had sent him word that there were five mortgages for thirty thousand dollars on the estate, and had trained a duck-gun from the hen-house to shoot him whenever he should look out of the window.

"I think," said Samyule, in great agitation, "that we had better flee while yet there is one whole car left on the Grand Southern Trunk Railroad. A meeting of Southern Conservative Democrats," says Samyule, uneasily, "is now being held on a lawn at the back of this chateau, to consider the advisability of hanging us this evening for the benefit of the Stonewall-Jackson-Monument Fund; and I really think we had better make a wicked flee while no man pursueth."

And we fled, my boy. We retired hastily to the nearest broken culvert; and when the next train ran off the track there, we got on board the one freight car left undemolished, and returned safely with the wounded to this city.

Is Southern property really being sold, with great sacrifice, to Northern capitalists at this present time? I think it is; I should say it was; the great sacrifice always going with the property and causing the Northern capitalist to wish he hadn't!

Not to dwell longer upon a subject which is so mercenary that I should show "nary" mercy for you did I pursue it longer, allow me to digress abruptly to the theatre of Impeachment, where another soliloquy for the defence is being delivered by the venerable Andrew Nelson.

"MR. CHIEF JUSTICE AND SENATORS," says this aged man, while slumber settles upon all around, "I have been busy in my profession of lawyer for twenty years, and have argued cases involving life, liberty, and the pursuit of happiness.

> ' How doth the little busy bee
> Improve each shining hour,
> And gather honey all the day
> From ev'ry opening flower !'

But I feel that all cases sink into insignificance when compared with this one. I am really too old, and have lived too much in the country, to argue this case. But I implore help from On High to make my mind, heart, and tongue, capable of keeping you awake for a few moments.

> "'Tis the voice of the sluggard,
> I hear him complain;
> 'You have woke me too soon,
> I must slumber again.'

If the President of the United States is indeed guilty of one tithe that has been charged against him, then I am willing to admit that he is a monster of such hideous mien that each particular hair does stand on end when he is seen. But who is this Andrew Johnson? Who is he, that you all come down upon him like quills upon a fretful porcupine? Who is he, —

> 'Come riddle me, riddle me rye,
> Two long ears and one great "I"?'

Go to the village of Greenville, East Tennessee, and inquire. See him a poor boy, unable to read or write, but yet industrious. He becomes a tailor, then an alderman, then a Congressman, and then a President. This is the man whom I hear accused of being apparently under the influence of Old Rye; of not caring sixpence for the Constitution; of betraying the blacks; of almost aspiring to be king, —

> 'Sing a song of sixpence,
> A pocket full of rye,
> Four and twenty blackbirds
> Cooked into a pie.
> When the pie was opened,
> The birds began to sing;
> Isn't this a pretty dish
> To set before a king?'"

Thus went on this aged man, introducing all the popular airs in order to secure attention; but none listened to his lay. *

* Appendix, 4.

When I came forth from the Capitol and looked upward again, there loomed the mighty Stomach once more in the sunset; there it was, my boy, as predominant as ever. Still repelling the thought that its immediate self could possibly be responsible for any ailing of the body-politic; still referring the Doctor with his harsh nostrums to the head, or the lungs, and permitting no ministrations to itself, save those of the Butler.

Yours, meditatively,
Orpheus C. Kerr.

LETTER IX.

BEING A VERACIOUS ACCOUNT OF THE UNPARALLELED MATCH AGAINST NATURE BY THE "AMERICAN PROOF-READER" AND THE "BOSTON MARVEL;" WITH ITS INEVITABLY TRAGICAL TERMINATION.

WASHINGTON, D. C., April 28, 1868.

It is a barbarism of our common nature, my boy, to take a morbid pleasure in unnatural exhibitions which imperil human life; and from the circus to the grave, man has ever the same heartless fondness for breakneck equestrian acts, and foolhardy attempts to read Presidents' Messages. It is highly probable that in the coming golden age, when Southerners shall be free from mortgages, Ireland all removed to the Sixth Ward of this country, and the freed-negro race happily supplied with seal rings and the right of suffrage, philanthropy will be at liberty to protest against that cruel popular taste which craves and encourages feats of deadly daring or endurance. Until then, however, there can be no difficulty in finding remunerative patronage for the temporizing suicide of the tight-rope, the walker of a thousand miles in a thousand hours, and the mad wretch who offers for a wager to ride twenty consecutive miles upon the Erie Railroad without a life-insurance policy. In such a state of things, we have no cause for surprise if desperate men are found willing to rescue themselves from want by recklessly overtasking nature's strength for the money to be made by it.

Since my last writing, a couple of needy unfortunates, in this city, have dared to trifle with the laws of life by entering into a match to read all the Impeachment speeches in succession,* without sleeping save at nights; and the consequence was, that two poor, emaciated creatures were presently lying upon hospital cots in fits of imbecile delirium, almost constantly maundering over such phrases as, — "Is this a court?" "Your honorable body;" and "The learned counsel."

The match commenced, my boy, in a patent cylindrical Glass and Lemon Repository, whither those Congressmen who have colds, repair to steep slices of the fruit in warm tumblers for their coughs; and thither went I, on several occasions, to view the hapless wretches at their task.

Both were strong, robustious men, of some previous practice in heavy reading. The first, who is known in sporting circles as "The American Proof-reader," corrected the proofs of four directories last year without the use of stimulants. And the second, whose admirers style him "The Boston Marvel," once read two articles in the "North American Review," at a sitting. Having learned these facts, I was inclined to regard the Marvel as the more severely-tested athlete of the twain; but overhearing a whisper from one of the knowing ones, that the

---

* These speeches, altogether, occupied over one hundred hours for their delivery.

Proof-reader had been practising upon the leaders in "The Nation," some weeks before, I finally gave him the preference.

The rash contestants were dressed in blue shirts, cotton drawers, and canvas shoes, as they were to walk incessantly while reading, in order to keep off sleep the more effectually; and their course extended around four billard-tables. Upon one of the latter sat the second or principal backer of each, with stimulants, bottles of hartshorn, and kettle-drums. On a long bench against the wall sat the time-keeper, with some hundred pounds of Impeachment speeches beside him, to be furnished to the readers as required; and near one of the tables stood a physician for the insane, to be at hand in case either foolhardy unfortunate should show symptoms of mental derangement in the course of the feat.

Promptly at the call of "Time!" the men started briskly together on the great opening speech of the Hon. Thaddeus Butler; their elbows pressed closely to their sides; the printed slip held firmly within ten inches of their eyes; and their pace almost a trot. At first they read very fast, and were neck-and-neck on the passage about the "intention of Our Fathers in framing the Constitution;" but upon reaching the first quarter-pole, where the question arises "whether this Senate is now sitting as a court, or a jury, or a coroner's inquest," the pace of the American Proof-reader became languid, and his eyelids gave signs of heaviness. His backer promptly ran alongside of him and applied a bottle of hartshorn to his nostrils, which roused him again; but the Boston Marvel had already reached the place where "the President is shown to have lost all dignity," and his friends grew quite boisterous in their triumph. Upon gaining the point where "it is not denied that the respondent has been a serious obstacle to reconstruction," he, too, however, lagged and yawned horribly, in his turn, compelling his backer to beat a drum in order to keep him awake. So that, at the close of the first day, the two men were about even, and were led to their beds upstairs in nearly equal states of exhaustion.

On the second day, both looked haggard, and gaped repeatedly at the mere sight of the speeches; yet they started off in fair style on the argument of the Hon. Andrew Curtis, and the betting was even until they had arrived at the juncture where "we will now call the attention of this honorable Court to the first of the foreign parliamentary trials cited by the honorable Managers." Here the American Proof-reader emitted a faint snore, and the Boston Marvel came near walking through a window in a doze. Drums were beaten, pistols fired, and rockets exploded, to keep the men awake; but, at the conclusion of the heat, both readers fell to the floor in a leaden sleep, and were thus carried to their beds.

The scenes on the following days were still more horrible, as each poor wretch made more Herculean efforts to struggle through the Hon. Thaddeus Boutwell and the

Hon. Andrew Nelson, without yielding to outraged nature's demand for half-hourly slumber. The men repeatedly fell, in utter exhaustion, and were picked up by attendants who rubbed them with oil, to loosen their minds, or beat drums and fumed their principals with hartshorn, to keep the faculties alive through eloquent passages. Reeling, and half-blind with intolerable weariness, the exhausted contestants went wildly into the speech of the venerable Nelson, and it was evident to all, that this would finish them. Over the questions "Who is he?" "Who is Andrew Johnson?" they stumbled piteously, with half-shut eyes; and at the first poetical quotation — "How does the little busy bee" — the Boston Marvel rolled under a billard-table in a swoon. Amid the beating of drums, firing of pistols, and showers of hartshorn, the American Proof-reader dragged himself painfully over the passage about "the Alta Vela case;" but at the second poetical quotation — "Come riddle me, riddle me, rye" — he threw up his hands, burst into a shrill laugh, and went down upon his back like a log.

They would have rubbed him with oil again, — those fiercely excited, heartless lookers-on, who cared not for two human lives if they could but win their bets, — they would have filled his nose with hartshorn and started him again on Williams, Stevens, and Evarts; but the physician for the insane would not permit it.

"No," said the physician, sternly; "I will not allow it. This great American Proof-reader is already so much weakened in his mind by these Impeachment speeches that I fear the result may be in-Senate-y. He is not strong enough to bear any more, and I shall order him and his opponent to the hospital."

•A deep silence fell upon the throng, while a party of attendants lifted the two victims of Impeachment from the ground preparatory to bearing them away; and it was heartbreaking to hear the hapless creatures feebly rave in the delirium produced by entire physical prostration. "Oh!" groaned the Boston Marvel, "I think I see the Common, and Ticknor & Fields' new bookshop through the trees. Am I, indeed, in heaven, and are the angels singing Mrs. Julia Ward Howe's poems to their golden harps? But no! what I took for eternity is Mr. Evarts' speech; and the angels are singing Nelson's poetical quotations! Is that Stanbery coming with another speech; and Bingham too? Save me from them! Impeach me and let me die!" The great American Proof-reader also struggled weakly with his bearers, and uttered a low wail, and says he: "No! no! I cannot correct the proof of any more directories to-night. But what am I saying? These are not directories,—they are twenty volumes of Impeachment speeches, with a map accompanying each. I have corrected the maps, which show that each speech extends to the last degree of longitude and has no parallels of platitude. Ask me no more, for I would sleep!"

Not being a really bad man at heart, my boy, I felt a guilty consciousness of having been in some way accessory

to this harrowing scene by attending as a thoughtless
spectator; and I penitently resolved to expiate my inhumanity by visiting and comforting the American Proof-
reader, in the hospital, instead of attending the Impeachment matinée. So, thither I went, like a masculine
Florence Nightingale, and was presently seated beside the
low pallet of one who, but a few days before, had been
exultant in health and reason. Now, however, he was sick
enough to be a principal Impeachment Manager, or leading Counsel for the Defence,* and there was no more coherence in his mutterings than in one of Emerson's lectures.
The physician for the insane had already administered one
of Timothy Titcomb's poems to him as an emetic, that he
might be enabled thereby to disgorge some of the heavier
words upon his stomach; but there had been so many
repetitions in the Impeachment speeches that it seemed as
though a blood-vessel might be broken before all danger
from tautology was over.

"Tell me," said I, anxiously, "what I can do to calm
and comfort this great American Proof-reader in his present
dreadful state, and thus partially atone for my own share
in the recent unnatural exhibition. Let me do something to
lull his George Francis Train style of raving, or the enemies of human reason will presently combine to make him
a European Correspondent of the "New York World."

The aged physician wrapt his saw, chisel, and gold watch
in a piece of brown paper again, and says he, —

* Manager Stevens and Counsel Stanbery were sick.

"I at first thought of amputating the os frontis and extracting some of the words from the orifice; but as he seems quieter now, I will wait awhile. What he needs most," says the physician, thoughtfully, "is present sleep. I will therefore leave three of the New York daily journals with you, and you may read to him a leading editorial from each."

Thus speaking, he left me; and, without another look at the moaning sufferer, I read aloud from the "Tribune"* the following able article, entitled

"IMPEACHMENT IS PEACE.

"From Maine to Philadelphia the ears of a nation of freemen are stretched to catch the first note of the fiat by which Andrew Johnson shall be ordered, in the name of the outraged American people, to return to that merited obscurity from which he was bloodily raised by the pistol of the assassin. When General Grant was recently in Philadelphia, he remarked audibly to a friend, that, upon the conviction and emulsion of the President depended the Peace of the whole country. Nor would any man deny such a self-evident fact, save, perhaps, Mr. Horatio Seymour, to whom the designation of Deliberate and Immeasurable Falsifyer has more than once been applied by

---

* This excellent moral journal is largely edited by gentlemen from Philadelphia, who miss no opportunity of improving the value of real estate in their native town, by making editorial mention of that growing place.

prominent citizens of Philadelphia. The United States Senate need hesitate no longer in its verdict."

Already the patient had sunk into a doze when I concluded this excellent "leader;" and I softly took up the "Times," * and read therefrom concerning what it called

"IN MEDIAS RES.

"While it cannot be denied that the sympathies of youth are all with the animated counsel for the defence, it must still be admitted that the grave admiration of meditative maturity accords no mean palm to the earnest pertinacity of some of the managers. Good taste may possibly take exception to one or two of Butler's turbulent invectives; yet we question whether more indulgence will be vouchsafed to the petulant parentheses of Mr. Nelson. As the case stands at present, we can only reprobate all attempts to prejudice a verdict not yet fully incubated; nor shall we countenance with our approval the attempt of any party

---

* In this skilful Conservative-Radical Dem-Republican morning journal, of July 16th, 1859, appeared a remarkable article on the French, Sardinian, and Austrian war in Italy, which said, —

"If we follow the windings of the Mincio, we shall find countless elbows formed in the elbows of the regular army, at places like Salianzi, Molini, and Borghetto."

And also, —

"After a battle of several hours' duration, the Sardinians at Goito gave way; and, if we follow up the course of the Mincio, we shall find innumerable elbows formed by the sympathy of youth."

Such is Conservative journalism in the United States.

to delay, or be indifferent to, a decision on which hang all the law and the profits."

A gentle snore smote my ear at the termination of the above discriminating expression of sentiment; but, to make my work complete, I grasped the "Herald," and read about

"RADICAL RUIN AND ITS REMEDY.

"Intent only upon elevating old Ben Wade to a temporary dictatorship, the Radical Jacobins are prepared to impeach even old Justice Chase, and fetter the hands of old General Grant. With old Thad Stevens as Secretary of State, and old Fred Douglas in the Treasury, we should soon witness all the excesses of old Robespierre repeated. To meet this emergency, let the Democratic party nominate old Admiral Farragut as their candidate for the Presidency, with old General Hancock for Vice-President."

Throwing aside this last paper, I looked at the American Proof-reader, and found that he not only slumbered soundly, but that he was also in a profuse perspiration. "He is safe!" whispered I, joyfully, to myself. "He is safe, despite the awful manner in which he has tempted Providence."

In an almost gleeful frame of mind, I was about to steal from the room, when the physician entered again, looking so gravely that I fairly caught my breath.

"He has had a narrow escape," muttered the man of medicine, glancing at the pallet.

"And how is the Boston Marvel?" asked I, quickly.

The Physician for the Insane turned his solemn eyes upon me, and pointed impressively upward.

"He is DEAD!"

Yours, speechlessly,
ORPHEUS C. KERR.

LETTER X.

MORALIZING UPON THE CERTAIN RESULT OF VICE-PRESIDENCY; GIVING THE CURIOUS EPITAPH OF A VICTIM OF ELOQUENCE; PRESENTING THE PRINCIPAL GEMS OF A GUANO MATINÉE; AND RECORDING THE ENTHUSIASM OF THE POPULACE OVER THE LAST OF THE IMPEACHMENT SPEECHES.

WASHINGTON, D. C., May 9, 1868.

AFTER having put on our spectacles, snuffed the candle, and perused the world's history, my boy, we cannot but perceive that vice, sooner or later, brings misery. It being a very late hour when we have finished the history, we debate within ourselves whether we had better go to bed and take a few years of sleep, or sit up for the brief remainder of the century and meditate upon that which our historical reading has taught us. Inasmuch as fully twenty-five pianos of cats have organized an angel-choir on the fences nearest our window, and a heavy shower of bootjacks has recently set in from the casements of seven unmarried gentlemen around the corner, we conclude to remain wakeful and ponder

THE WORLD'S HISTORY.

A baby smiling on a mother's knee,
A faint ray breaking o'er an Eastern sea,
A green leaf peeping from a root deep set,
A candle waxen, and unlighted yet.

SMOKED GLASS.

A school-boy mimicking a lark's clear cry,
A red flush blazoning a morning sky,
A frail twig bending to a zephyr's thought,
A candle twinkling with a spark just caught.

A lover kneeling to a maiden fair,
A sun all golden in a cloudless air,
A bud slow swelling on a fragrant bough,
A candle crested with a white flame now.

A soldier fighting for a prize ne'er gained,
A spot of fever on a zenith stain'd,
A branch low drooping with a fruit half sear,
A candle gutt'ring with a jaundiced blear.

A miser gloating at a coffer's brim,
A gray gleam ending in a twilight dim,
A dry leaf crackling in a wintry fall,
A candle smoking to a shadow'd wall.

A dotard gasping in a parson's ear,
A pale star dying in a storm-cloud near,
A tall tree loosening a clasp'd root-hand,
A candle flick'ring at a wick's last strand.

A shadow resting on a square of white,
A sun's ghost walking in a noon of night,
A prone trunk hollow to a worm's vile tread,
A candle wasted and a mortal dead.

As for yourself, my boy, I judge, from your general conversation on politics, that there is far more gas than candle about you; and, consequently, your share of this history need not alarm you. But, as I was saying before, the man of striking originality of thought will derive therefrom the idea, that vice, sooner or later, brings misery; and at once take measures to have it inserted in the "Lady's Book" as his own great American composition. When we consider the lilies of the valley, — that they toil not, neither do they spin; and yet, that Solomon, in all his glory, was not arrayed like one of these; we may possibly feel inclined to side with Solomon for refraining from such spring fashions as would have been likely to subject him to the care of the police. I know several wealthy Southerners, who, in consequence of innumerable mortgages and certain not remote exploits of our military vandals, are arrayed so much like lilies of the valley that they feel obliged to lie in bed all day until bathing-time comes. But then, again, when we consider Andrew Johnson, and remember that vice sooner or later brings misery, we can scarcely refrain from reprobating such an extraordinary addiction to vice as finally tempted him to become a Vice-President. Save for such uncommon viciousness, he might now be a profane and respected member of Congress, calling all the other members by the most awful and amusing names, and assisting them to impeach somebody for having no friends. Instead of that, however, we find him the guilty cause of over one hundred hours of speeches; all of which have fallen upon our distracted country, while she is yet writhing under the recollection of Mr. Raymond's address at the Dickens' dinner. Thus it is that vice sooner or later brings misery, and occasions such death, even, as that of the Boston Marvel.

Early this morning I strolled out to the place where they have laid the poor Marvel, and was pleased to find erected over his resting-place a neat slab bearing the following inscription, —

Hic Jacet
MANTON MARVEL
OF BOSTON.

> Impeachment Speeches wrought his hapless fate;
> BUT-LE'RNing CURT-IS to appease his shade:
> The BOUT-WELL ended, 'NEL'-S'ON rang for him —
> Eye GROES-BECKlouded at the end he made.
> When LO'- 'GAN he, with WILL-I- AM-sure, to read,
> He thought each speech to scan, what EVAR'TS length;
> But quickly found (iS'T EVEN-so indeed?)
> That half of them would quite exhaust one's strength.
> For birth to " hub "-BING-HAMlet he was debtor;
> And Here he's buried.   Few STAN'-BERYing better.*

These few simple tributary lines had been written evidently, by some humble friend, whose spelling was defect-

---

* The speakers for the prosecution were Messrs. Butler, Boutwell, Logan, Williams, Stevens, and Bingham. For the defence, Messrs. Curtis, Groesbeck, Evarts, and Stanbery. It is scarcely necessary to say that the Epitaph should read, —

> Impeachment Speeches wrought his hapless fate;
> But learning curt is to appease his shade;
> The bout well ended, knell soon rang for him —
> Eye grows beclouded at the end he made.
> When low 'gan he, with will, I am sure, to read,
> He thought each Speech to scan, what ever 'ts length;
> But quickly found (is't even so, indeed ?)
> That half of them would quite exhaust one's strength.
> For birth to " hub "-bing hamlet he was debtor;
> And Here he's buried.   Few stand burying better.

ive; but they had a touching pathos for me, and made me whisper again to myself, Vice-President sooner or later brings misery.

On another occasion, as I walked thoughtfully along a retired byway near the Capitol, philosophically pondering the same sad conclusion, my attention was attracted to a figure sitting upon a wayside-stone, its back towards me. It was bending eagerly forward to a wooden hitching-post just before it. Its soft black hat rested upon the very back of its head after the manner of some sable Thomas-cat clinging to a bedpost; and its hands hastily shuffled and cut a pack of greasy cards for the apparent accommodation of an invisible partner. Stealing closer to this absorbed apparition, I quickly recognized the Conservative Kentucky Chap, and also noted that he was talking excitedly to the hitching-post.

"Hem!" says he, dealing two here and two there, and simultaneously making a pass of two kings and an ace up his coat-sleeve. "Kentucky will play you just one game of Bluff, Mr. Post, to see if her former tailor, A. Johnson, will be acquitted or convicted. If I win, it is in favor of the respondent. If you win, the verdict will be otherwise. You play first, and I 'see' you, and go five cents better."

"Well done, my private Morrissey!" says I, tapping him on the shoulder. "Your manner of deciding a great national case might well be adopted by one of those fastidious Senators whose consciences are said to make them uncertain about their verdict."

Hastily leaping to his feet, and slipping the cards out of sight into a convenient pocket, the Kentucky chap eyed me sorrowfully, and says he, —

"The old rye-crop of Kentucky is greatly retarded and depreciated by the vast quantity of milk and water daily poured out by the Impeachment Jacobins; and nothing but an acquittal can improve the market."

"You are unduly depressed," says I, sympathetically, "because all the reliable morning journals have been driven by excess of speeches to tear their hair, and predict a future of inexpressible woe and eloquence. Come with me to the House of Congress, where a guano matinée is now being held. It will cheer your mind; and as we've both got our old clothes on, we needn't mind a little dirt."

Bowing a mute assent, and fervently grasping my hand, the afflicted chap permitted me to lead him as I listed; and we proceeded to that great national hall of legislation where statesmen are "native and to the manure born." In the gallery were quite a number of spectators, dressed in bad clothes for the occasion, and protected by a barricade of opened umbrellas and upreared benches against the time when the mud should begin to fly. These we joined, and were at once interested in a great scene between the Hon. Anasta Puddle, and the Hon. Mr. Bottler.*

---

* Passage-at-arms in the House, between Messrs. Brooks and Butler concerning the Alta Vela (guano island) business.

The Hon. Anasta Puddle threw a handful of guano at the Hon. Mr. Bottler, and says he, "I deem it my duty as a member of the incorruptible Democratic Organization, to charge yonder impure being with the loathsome crime of endeavoring to intimidate the President into giving all the guano known to the birds of the air to certain corrupt parties."

The Hon. Mr. Bottler used both his hands to throw guano all over the Hon. Anasta Puddle, and says he, "This fellow, Puddle, is mad at me because I know about his trying once to swindle one of his partners. He is a disgusting object."

The Hon. Anasta Puddle hurled a pailful of guano at the Hon. Mr. Bottler, and says he, "I regret to say that I am cognizant of several burglaries committed by this creature, Bottler, and cannot but mourn my further knowledge of his earlier attempt to work domestic misery in the family of a bricklayer. I demand a committee to investigate his subsequent efforts to commit arson."

The Hon. Pignatius Wallowly next arose to protest against a recent newspaper letter of the Hon. Mr. Washwoman; and says he, "The infamous office-beggar to whom I allude has made certain charges against me in a letter, and I hereby hold up the unclean wretch to general loathing. Why, sir, this incredible wallower in infamy comes here with a record recking from—" (Here the Court allowed the speaker to write the sentence on a slip of paper, as it was unfit for print). "And do we not all

Drama of the period. Guano Matinée.

know that this polluted reptile is sole owner of the candidate for the next Presidency? Do we not all know that this unparalleled dabbler and frequent betrayer of—" (The Court permitted the speaker to commit the remark to writing, as it would not do for print). "Yet this same gentleman, this same person who, in a game of euchre with his own brother, would use marked cards—"

HON. MR. POLLTAX, Speaker of the House, decided that the last remark was unparliamentary.

The HON. MR. WASHWOMAN arose calmly, and says he, "The party may go on all day if he chooses. I scorn to notice the impotent drivel of a—" (Witness was suffered by the Court to pencil the name on a piece of paper, as it was unsuitable for publication). "I have plainly said, in the letter to which he takes exception, that he once fled from his native city under a false name, because he had been detected in—" (The Court directed deponent to write the remainder of the remark on a slip of foolscap, as it was not adapted to public print.) "And now let the party go on."

The HON. PIGNATIUS was sorry if he had said anything unparliamentary, and demanded a Committee to ascertain what day would be most convenient for the execution of the Hon. Mr. Washwoman. If the proposition was not out of order, he begged leave to invite all present to go out and take the Test-oath with him.*

*Appendix, 5.

Amid the great enthusiasm naturally produced by this pleasant termination of what had been a somewhat agitated debate, the Kentucky Chap and I hurriedly repaired to the nearest bathing establishment, where, after we had carefully bathed, and had the splashes scraped from our coats, we took different paths. In a much improved frame of mind, the pride of Kentucky started toward Pennsylvania Avenue, while I designed a brief stroll about the Capitol grounds for the quieter meditation upon the great truths we had just heard. Plunged in a delicious reverie, I had but commenced my walk, when sounds of loud cheering from the theatre of Impeachment caused me to hastily enter that solemn temple and view the culminating pageant.

The Hon. Thaddeus Bingham had just concluded his touching remarks detrimental to the respondent. He had just finished his scathing exposure of an accidental President whose lack of all decorum in public speaking has justly subjected him to Impeachment by an outraged Congress; and the assembled populace were cheering the consummate artist. Such disagreeable sounds, however, were unseemly in such a place, inasmuch as they awoke thirteen aged Senators from much-needed slumber, and jarred the spectacles from the noses of two venerable counsels for the defence.

The Chief Justice tore off his night-cap and threw it at a deaf chap in the gallery who had not heard the call for Silence, and was still stamping and clapping horribly;

and says he, "The police will please remove the galleries, as it is impossible for the Senate to sleep amid such confusion."

Thus, at the mandate of arbitrary power, we were all driven forth from our dormitories into the pitiless air. Amongst the throng was the Mackerel Chaplain, and says I to him, —

"Who shall think, after such a popular ovation as this to a native orator, that American eloquence is declining?"

"My good young friend," says the chaplain, shaking his head, "it will ever remain a question in men's minds, whether the late applause was a tribute to native eloquence, or a free people's irrepressible delight at the assured termination of the last of the Impeachment Speeches."

Yours, undecidedly,
ORPHEUS C. KERR.

LETTER XI.

TAKING A HOPEFUL VIEW OF THE FUTURE OF AMERICAN ART; AFFORDING VALUABLE HINTS TO THE COMING GREAT HISTORICAL PAINTER; AND SHOWING HOW A SUDDEN AND UNPRECEDENTED OUTBREAK OF MORALITY CAUSED A LAMENTABLE "HITCH" IN THE GREAT FINAL TRANSFORMATION SCENE OF THE MAJESTIC DRAMA OF IMPEACHMENT.

WASHINGTON, D. C., May 16, 1868.

As we excitedly gaze through a piece of Smoked Glass, my boy, upon the dazzling artistic resources of this distracted country, and contemplate the National Academy of Design, the American Water-Color Society, and the House and Sign Painters' Protective Union, we find ample encouragement for a hope that the æsthetical future will develop some great native wizard of the ladder, pencil, and brush, whose canvas shall worthily portray a few of the more awful and chaste events of our intoxicated national history. Having paid twenty-five cents admission fee to the old lady at the door, and taken checks for their canes from the decayed artist's male orphan in the vestibule, our grandchildren will walk in to survey the pictures after the manner of dispassionate critics. "Oh!"—they will softly whisper to each other, as they stand affably before the paintings, and assume that thoughtfully scowling expression of countenance which is equally indicative of painters' colic, and a cultivated knowledge of the fine arts — "Oh! how grand must these Impeachment scenes have been to those who beheld them in reality! How much must they have reminded their living spectators of the sublime Senatorial pageants of ancient Rome!" After saying which, and casually recognizing a few spring bonnets of their acquaintance, our grandchildren will probably step out together for a moment to obtain a glass of water and a clove for their colds.

The strict utilitarian will sneer at this artistic anticipation as the mere vision of an enthusiast; the mere wild speculation of some dreamy worshipper of Titian and Rubens, whose sanguine temperament has been unduly fired by an infatuated adoration of the glorious frescoes upon the walls of the Capitol and the sides of the East Broadway omnibuses. But I beg leave to make a pass at the strict utilitarian with a broomstick, and calmly inform him, in the gossipy language of the "Tribune," that he is a perjured traitor to Impeachment, a revolting object to his constituents, and a source of permanent regret to his Maker. Upon a coarser subject I should feel justified in using stronger terms; but art is still a delicate exotic with us, and we must not attempt to dragoon its disbelievers into unity with us by assailing them with violent abuse. I simply repeat, then, that the strict utilitarian is an accursed renegade to all that preserves from the loathing of his fellow-beings any person differing on any subject from myself.

My belief in the exciting future of American Art is NOT

based upon the frescoes on the walls of the Capitol and the sides of the New York omnibuses. No, sir! The members of Congress from my State may unanimously call upon me to resign, or request me to refrain from voting, but I must still adhere to my honest convictions. Great outside pressure being brought to bear upon me, I may, indeed, admit that I once noticed on the interior panels of an Erie railroad-carriage a series of pink-and-blue Scriptural paintings, which showed what native art may yet do toward preparing people's minds for a roll down an embankment, and an accompanying fatal roast in a burning sleeping-car. I may also admit, that much of the finer statuary in and around the Capitol bids fair to find ample appreciation in every American household during the coming years; mothers saying to their refractory children, "Don't cry now, my dear, or the statue of Benjamin Franklin will come after you." "Go right to sleep, like a good boy, Johnny, or the equestrian figure of General Jackson will catch you." But none of these great works are responsible for my artistic faith in the future.

A true friend of mine (that is, one who tells me of my faults, and seems really to regret that he has none of his own), who lives here in a frame house, got a young artist-acquaintance to do the front of his residence last week, and, as I watched the progress of the *chef d'œuvre*, I could not but feel high hopes that the impressive splendors of Impeachment might indeed find a worthy limner at last.

Mounted on a ladder which was not more than twice tall

enough for the edifice, and armed with a brush not much larger than his head, the gifted young painter laid on his touches with a boldness and breadth not always limited by the mere width of the house. It must be admitted that he got nearly as much paint upon the ladder and his own clothes as upon the residence, and that, in reaching after some nice effects of light and shade along the gutter-pipe, he produced quite a picturesque and irregular white border on the edge of the red-brick house next door; but the way that he threw chiaro oscuro into the shutters, and painted clean through a pane of glass to the back of a rosewood chair standing inside, was enough to show his genius. And then, when he finally descended to the sidewalk, which looked by this time as though a violent snow-storm were stuck fast to it, and began working-up the stoop in straw-color, I was amazed at the facility of his method. Like other native artists, his drawing was not always exactly correct, — at times he drew his brush so far over the edge that some of the straw-color ran down into the area, and about a pint of it must have passed between the door and sill into the hall, — yet his middle-distance was good, and the place where he rubbed off the paint by sitting down on it to tie his shoe would not be noticed on a dark night. Being no member of the pre-Raphaelite school, and scorning that mechanical minuteness of petty detail which belongs rather to the photographer's drudge than to the true artist, he neglected to paint behind a towel hanging from one of the upper windows, and also left a few bare streaks up near the caves, but, then, to secure harmony of effect, he painted the door-plate and door-knob with the greatest care.

In the afternoon, my friend returned home from Impeachment, and, after slipping down upon the white lead on the sidewalk and getting his vest, coat, and hat tastefully touched up with turpentine and straw-color, stared critically at the great work.

"Dear me," says he, with unreasonable hypercriticism, "isn't that place up there, by the towel, a little too sketchy?"

The sensitive young artist pushed him impatiently aside with his paint-brush, and says he, —

"Do you expect to examine a great painting by standing close enough to touch it with your nose? Just step off to the proper distance, — a couple of blocks, say, — and you'll see the difference."

My friend retired a couple of blocks for the purpose; but quickly returned in great agitation, and says he, —

"From that distance the house doesn't look as though it had been painted at all."

"Exactly!" says the young artist, triumphantly. "The perfection of art is to conceal art. I'll leave the ladder standing here five or six days, and send in my bill immediately." And he shook hands with us with the greatest good feeling, and promptly retired with the pots to his Academy of Painting.

His work, my boy, was a bold Sketch, a strong Study, rather than a strictly-finished composition; and what I at first took for his signature in the lower right-hand corner, has since proved to be the sign of a Dutch boot-maker keeping shop in the basement; but the young artist is destined to rise (especially when he has a ladder with him), and, as he is particularly noted for his Varnishing also, we may well believe that the man destined to pictorialize Impeachment for posterity is not far off. The man must be really great with VARNISH, you see, or the sublime historical work may be regarded by posterity as altogether too shallow-looking and crude to be tolerated by respectable notice.

As it is unquestionably a duty of the contemporaneous historian to give the future artist certain vivid hints for his canvas, I take the liberty of insinuating that last Monday and Tuesday afternoons offered fine opportunities for sketching, and that some vigorous "whitewashing" was even attempted on the spot. Art, however, has its separate departments; and if the inspired whitewasher shall also be required to touch-up some of the principal figures in the great historical Impeachment picture of the future, it is to be hoped that the gifted young painter and varnisher will not grudge a reasonable share of the honors to his brother-artist. Many of our very greatest public men are already known to prefer whitewash to natural colors in such portraits of themselves as are taken for posterity; and, aside even from the admitted necessity of this branch of art in the depiction of such eminent historical personages, its practical encouragement by all true philanthropists cannot fail to aid notably in the elevation of the freed-negro race, many of whose members are its ablest exponents.

To both branches of art, then, I may intimate, that a picture representing a massive lump of white sugar in an elevated background, and about ten thousand agitated horse-flies swarming at it in the fore and middle ground, will convey a reliable idea of the majestic Theatre of Impeachment on the afternoons I have named. A general and particular understanding that the great final Transformation Scene of the exciting play was to have a private rehearsal on Monday, preparatory to its triumphant production at the Tuesday matinée, caused all the unemployed persons in the United States to visit this city without further confusion; and, as I looked down from my window at Willard's upon the dense throng of amusement-seekers in the street, I could not help saying to myself, after the manner of Xerxes,—

"Of all these myriads, not one will be alive in a hundred years from now! None live more than a hundred years, except revolutionary veterans and poll-parrots. Even now, some five or six Senators are seriously sick from Impeachment Speeches. The thought is melancholy, and I'll just step down to the bar-room and see if there are any letters for me from Jamaica or Santa Cruz."

But the surging throng in the hallways caught me as I descended, and I was summarily swept out-doors upon the Avenue, just in time to hear the remarks of the venerable Miss P. Hen; who had arrived hastily from New York expressly to witness the great Transformation Scene, and was waving her blue cotton umbrella in a spirited harangue to the populace. Miss P. Hen is the author of the most reliable History of the War ever delivered to subscribers at four dollars a volume, besides being celebrated for bailing out the recent well-known Southern Confederacy; and says she,—

"The great Transformation Scene will satisfy everybody, and be universally accepted by the press and public as the most splendid spectacle of the age. A. Johnson is transformed into a private citizen; B. Wade is turned into the King of Fairy-Land, and all the seven-thirties are changed into five-twenties. One of our great machinists, named Trumbull, is probably the most ingenious man ever known, and also deserves credit as the author of that immortal Civil Rights Act which permits colored men to go behind the scenes and—"

Here a well-informed chap came tearing frantically along from the majestic Theatre of Impeachment, and says he,—

"There's a hitch in the rehearsal of the Transformation Scene, my friends! Trumbull refuses to perform; because, he says, that theatricals are immoral."

Miss P. Hen made a pass at him with her blue cotton umbrella, and says she,—

"As every enemy of decency and morality remarks, Trumbull is the most ingenious man ever known; but outraged public sentiment points at him the withering finger of scorn, and the coming ages shall regard him as a noxious insect. Oh!" says Miss P. Hen, with wild emotion, "I feel that I could tear his eyes out!"

Turning sadly from sight of the gifted lady's tears, and edging slowly around a group of solid Boston men, who were committing an assault with carpet-bags upon another machinist, named Grimes, who was also suspected of having moral scruples against the drama, I came suddenly upon that haughty Southerner, Loyola Munchausen, who, in his surtout of French-Yoke Shirt, and Spring-overcoat of Water-Proof Awning, was malevolently offering bets against the success of the great Transformation Scene. He had left his organ and monkey at home in the suburban hen-house where he now resides; but I noticed two or three new business-cards pasted in the advertising panels of the half a boot-leg which he wears as a dress-hat; and says he, —

"Here you are, now, ten mortgages to five that the Transformation Scene don't work. Here you are: first and second mortgages on improved Southern real-estate. Ten to five that the great Transformation don't come off to-morrow."

Before I could salute him, there was a fresh excitement right behind me, where the irascible Miss P. Hen had 'lighted upon Fessenden, a third machinist, whose moral compunctions would not allow him to take final part in the immoral drama, and was indignantly beating him over the head with her blue cotton umbrella. "Oh!" says she to him, "you nasty thing!" And she stuck the ferule of her umbrella into his ear, and began spanking him with one of her shoes.*

And when the memorable Tuesday came, and it was really announced to the vast audience of the Impeachment matinée, that, in consequence of a defect in the complicated machinery, the great Transformation Scene must be deferred until Saturday, it actually seemed as though the dramatic public were bent upon having the Scene, even though it were given separately as merely a Farce.

Under the supervision of the incensed P. Hen, a public indignation meeting was immediately called, whereat it was unanimously resolved, that those machinists who were moral should either at once resign all employment and go to the Poorhouse, or be adjudged guilty of corruption, tergiversation, and inexpressible iniquity.

These, my boy, are a few of the points to which I would call the especial attention of the future great historical painters of this distracted country; trusting that varnish and whitewash will combine to make the pictures a refinement upon the originals,

Yours, sketchingly,
ORPHEUS C. KERR.

---

* " Beneath the rule of men entirely great,
  The P. Hen is mightier than the Seward."—BULWER.

LETTER XII.

NARRATING THE SUDDEN JOURNEY OF OUR CORRESPONDENT AND OTHERS TO THE SOUTH ON A MISSION OF RECONSTRUCTION; ILLUSTRATING THE USUAL GYMNASTIC PERILS OF AMERICAN RAILROAD TRAVEL; AND PORTRAYING HOW THE WRITER AND CAPTAIN VILLIAM BROWN, ESKEVIRE, WERE RECEIVED BY A RENOWNED CONFEDERACY.

CHIPMUNK COURT HOUSE, May 20, 1868.

THE Human Mind! — what a marvellous, commonplace, firm, unstable possession it is! The more we have of it to show, the greater is our envy of Shakespearian Commentators, Native Dramatists, Congressmen, and others, who possess merely that piece of mind which passeth show. Mine, my boy, is an inquiring mind, — that is to say, it ventilates itself in quires, — and, having grown weary of those Impeachment splendors which once it doated on, now asks itself, What next?

Inspiring me to smoke my piece of glass anew, it also directs me to turn that reliable safety-lens Southward; and, in obedience to the hint, I have even secured the appointment of National Stenographer to a Reconstructing Expedition lately organized for a Confederate clime, and now beg leave to propose a suitable prefatory sentiment, after the manner of all great historians.

Peace, meek-eyed Peace, has cut its snowy pigeonwings over the recent Southern tracks of Federal carnage, and our beloved country reels more mighty and prosperous from the late sanguinary affair than writhing Europe cares to admit. How beautiful is the spectacle, as we view it through a piece of Smoked Glass! How sublime a thing it is to see a million of strategic troops turning tranquilly from the tented field, and selling Newtown pippins on the ferry-boats! How ennobling it is to think that the very beings who were once brass-buttoned brigadiers, and drank success to the good cause in many a fiercely-contested bottle, are now applying in large numbers for admission to the bar kept by Themis!

'Tis sweet, my native land, to behold thine exhibition of so much majestic shape to the world; and all will ecstatically black thy boots, save affrighted Albion, and that imperial Gaul whose not remote purchase of our iron-clad "Dunderberg" * may yet make us wish that we hadn't made such French-ship.

Toning this sentiment to the more dulcet register of my fine organ (which I find to be the name for "voice," in the admirable musical criticisms of all our excellent morning journals), I expressed it to the Conservative Kentucky Chap, the other day, in an ante-room of the White House, where we stood waiting our turn to take a parting pardon with the Executive before departing on our several Government salaries.

Merely stepping aside for a moment, while a large-sized

* Now known as the "Rochambeau" of the Imperial navy.

Confederacy, on his way to take a pardon, made a cheerful pass with his bowie-knife at a one-armed Federal hireling near the wall, the Conservative Kentucky Chap pulled on a pair of yellow kid gloves, and says he, —

"'Tis sweet, indeed, to see our native land thus rising like a Felix from her ashes, and causing all the iron-clads of nature to tremble horribly together at Cherbourg and Spithead; but Kentucky far prefers the pageant of these Confederacies, now forgiving their recent Vandal foes, and taking pardon at the same table with him who was once their tailor." *

Here the Conservative Kentucky Chap accepted an apology from the haughty Virginian, who had accidentally knocked his hat over his eyes in an attempt to hit an adjacent crippled Hessian with his cane, and ate a hickory nut from the lunch-basket of a female Confederacy in front of him.

"Very true, my discriminating Von Bismarck," said I, sagely; "and I doubt not the forgiving nature of these sunny men expects to meet in return a disposition for giving them — anything they ask!"

"Hem!" says the Conservative Kentucky Chap, severely, as he moved hastily aside to let a Confederacy of much collar get his shoes polished by a member of our national conservative organization. "Hem!" says the

---

* It may be remembered that President Johnson's stronger demonstrations against Congress brought multitudes of ex-rebel pardon-seekers to the White House.

Kentucky chap, "you possess a radical soul, incapable of appreciating that noble sect of reconstructed planters with whom Kentucky is connected by marriage."

Cowering under his just rebuke, and thinking that, after all, I should be as well without a pardon so late in the afternoon, I shook hands with him, and then respectfully begged my way through all the Southern States to the front door, from whence I sped to the railroad depot, where Captain Villiam Brown and the Conic* Section of the late unconquerable Mackerel Brigade were to start with me for Chipmunk Court House, in storied Acsomac.

We were going by rail to reconstruct that sunflower of chivalry, Captain Munchausen; and we took to him, as a Provisional Governor, his elder brother, Loyola Munchausen, whose unflinching fidelity to the Union, in not taking arms for the South while laid up with typhus fever and inflammatory rheumatism, had very justly procured for him this appointment. It is by thus encouraging the loyal element of a sunny clime that we unite justice with magnanimity, and astonish Professor Goldwin Smith, of Oxford.

"Well, my wizard of the sword," said I to Villiam, as I espied that unpromoted warrior on the platform of a car, giving directions as to the disposal of his property to an attorney of his acquaintance, "is the Provisional aboard, and all right for starting?"

* The Mackerel "Conic" Section is so called by reason of its novel strategical tendency to assume the shape of a *cone* when going into action, the attenuated apex being toward the enemy.

"Yes, my fren'," said Villiam, handing his watch to the attorney, and sadly intimating that it was to be sent to his poor mother; "yes," says Villiam, "he's holding his breath on a seat by himself, and trying to be cam."

"Ah!" said I, vainly endeavoring to appear unmoved, "where are we expected to have our first engagement?"

"Just below here, my fren'," says Villiam, cutting off a lock of his hair for the attorney, "where a couple of rails are broken."

Too much affected to say more, we went into the car reserved for officers and civilians, and took a seat together, with our hands interclasped. Thus we sat; and, while the train was waiting for a speculative surgeon to come aboard, an agent of a Yankee "Accident Insurance Company" introduced a street-minstrel with a harp, who played and sang this harmless

BIT OF RAILLERY.

Botsy Bacon, dearest one,
    Lay your head upon my shoulder;
Will you go and be a nun,
    When your lover's hand is colder?

Will his mangled last remains
    Win from you a tear of pity? —
Oh, that other things than trains
    Took us to a neighboring city!

Wildly gazed she in my face,
    Crying, as she clung about me,
"Bobby, in the name of grace,
    Go away you sha'n't without me!

"Why, I thought you only meant,
　Just a business trip to make it;
Yet you seem on death intent; —
　Have you stole my heart to break it?

"Wherefore speak of death at all;
　Aren't you coming back to-morrow?
Let me some physician call; —
　What has crazed you, joy or sorrow?"

Betsy, darling — low I spoke —
　Don't you know by rail I'm going?
Ev'ry train there's something broke,
　By the daily paper's showing.

'Tis as sure as sure can be
　That some accident will happen;
Likely the first bridge we see
　Will give way and let us slap in.

Or a train of freight we'll strike,
　Or another train run into;
Count on life, with death so like? —
　Well you know 'twould be a sin to!

Sadly droop'd her pretty head,
　Like a lily rudely shaken;
"If for life you care," she said,
　"Stay at home, and save your Bacon!"

O sudden Death! At any time thou seemest to us the most terrible of earthly ills, save when Mr. Tupper brings out a new book; but how supernaturally malignant dost thou appear when we have to buy the tickets for our own funeral, and die standing on our heads between two mutilated brakemen.

"Hum!" says Villiam, thoughtfully, just as the train began to move; "are those the marbles of my childhood which mine eyes behold?"

I looked to the car floor, as he spoke, and beheld certain little figured glass balls, as they appeared to be, rolling loosely around; but, upon picking one up, I found it to be a human eye.

"Conductor," said I, calmly as I could, to a being attached to his watch by a large chain, who was waltzing solemnly down the aisle and doing the ticket trick, — "conductor," said I, "what mean these?"

"Why," says the conductor, pleasantly, "you see the cars haven't been swept out since that last little affair we had with the night express from Pinchtown." Here the affable conductor took up an eye, and says he, "If the crystal of that one wasn't broken, it would make a neat scarf-pin!"

Just at this moment, the engaging conductor quickly ascended to the top of the car, and put his head through the ventilator, and all the gentlemen in the seats adjacent joined me in sitting upon Captain Villiam Brown.

For we had had a spirited skirmish with a milk train, and had killed two drovers and a lozenge-boy.

"You see," said the polite conductor, coming down, and continuing the conversation, "when you have eyes only, you can't do much else than use them for scarf-pins; but when you have a few good legs, five or six hands that have come off clean, and as many tops of heads as would fill a small basket, the directors let you sell them to the medical students, for the company, and pay a fair commission to you."

The really agreeable conductor now darted through the length of the car, and placed his head through the top of the door, and four fat women and the Provisional Governor went to bed upon Villiam and me.

For we had had a sharp time on the right with a broken bridge, and wounded twelve Mackerels and the baggage-master.

"It must be plain to everybody," observed the genial conductor, coming back with his collar-bone broken, and resuming the interview, "that the leg and hand business will hardly pay you sometimes; for I have known whole weeks to pass without giving you anything more than a couple of dozen fingers, and a few poorly-executed knee-pans, which don't pay you for taking them to the medical college."

It was at this moment that the amiable conductor went very swiftly and stood upon his head behind the stove, and Villiam stretched himself at full length from a pink bonnet to a large "chignon."

For we had had a brilliant charge down a bank, and scalded three brakemen and a conductor.

"Some people might imagine," said the lively conductor, not minding his broken arms, and regaining the thread of his discourse, "that you might make something out of the feet and shoulder-blades you sometimes get; but the feet are apt to be too much crushed to pay, and so many shoulder-blades are brought to market from the Western trains, on which a great many elderly maiden ladies travel, that they are a perfect drug."

Upon which the thoroughly fascinating conductor vanished magically behind the half of the car-floor which arose between him and us, and Villiam and I retired over the top of the water-cooler.

For we had had a stirring affair with a broken tie, and rolled nine women and a quarter-master into one vigntipede.

Captain Villiam Brown removed the cover of the water-cooler from his head, where it had rested like a helmet, and says he, —

"Who shall care for mother now?"

"Cheer up, my blue and gold Achilles," said I, extricating my left thigh from the side of the car, and noticing with satisfaction that we had just run over a cow with safety; "cheer up, for we approach the place where awaits us the flower of chivalry!"

"Ah!" says Villiam, taking his will from an inner pocket, and pinning it to his coat collar, so that it might be easily seen by those who should find the upper part of his body, — "ah!" says he, softly, "train up a man in the way he should go, and he will not live to be old enough to depart from it. That is," says Villiam, explainingly, "if the train is on a railroad appertaining to the United States of America."

This sagacious remark of Villiam suggested to me that the "train up" in a man's case, like the "train up" in a child's, not unfrequently owed its mishaps to a misplaced switch; and I was about to convey the idea to Villiam, in the unstudied phraseology of our more serious comic journals, when we both went up like rockets into the air.

For we had had something of a brush with the exploding boiler of the locomotive, and had experienced what an ungrammatical person might denominate the last rose of summer.

"Hum!" says Villiam, from the top of a pine tree; "is this Chipmunk Court House?"

"It must be, my bird of Mars," murmured I, from the upper branches of a horse-chestnut.

Here a dreadful groan burst from Provisional Governor Munchausen, who was seated on the chimney of a deserted house beside the track, and says he, "Do my spectacles relate a falsehood, or is that really a human being up yonder?"

It was the figure of the engaging conductor, impaled upon a lightning-rod surmounting a lofty flag-staff, and striking feebly out with his hands and feet, after the manner of a fly on a pin. As we gazed, there came down a soft voice of solicitation, and it said, "Tick-ets!"

"Ah!" says Villiam, "his name is Tickets!"

Here the friendly conductor wriggled impatiently, and held down a hand toward us, and says he, —

"TICK-ETS!"

After which, he immediately folded up, and we felt that his spirit had fled to its native depot.

Luckily for us, my boy, Captain Munchausen now arrived at the scene, from his native palace, to pick out a few remains of such friends as might have come on the train; and as we came down the trees, and noticed nearly all the Conic Section coming down from other trees around, he nodded the woollen stocking which served him as a cap, and says he, —

"Having been overpowered by superior numbers, I am prepared to be reconstructed, and accept the temporary protection of your armed ruffians."

Villiam endeavored to draw his good sword, Escalibar; but, finding that exquisitely tempered weapon too much bent to come out of the scabbard, he remembered the terrifying effect of the word "Sirrah!" as found in all our absorbing weekly journals of aristocratic romance, and says he, —

"Peace, sarah!"

Captain Munchausen superciliously thrust his hands into his pockets, quite forgetful that all his knuckles came visibly through in front, and says he, —

"Let the Union meeting proceed to organize, after the wishes of our noble President."

Hereupon the Provisional Governor at once mounted an

inverted pail, and addressed the vast assemblage in the following speech, —

"FELLOW-CITIZENS OF ACCOMAC,—Four years of heroic war and glorious self-sacrifice, for a wicked cause still dear to every freeman's heart, having failed for the present to attain our independence, let us rejoice at the restoration of the beloved old Union, under our noble President, and return to it full of forgiveness for the present!"

Here the meeting was for a moment disturbed, by Captain Munchausen's involuntary discharge of a pistol at a Mackerel corporal, who was accidentally looking at him like a conqueror; but order was quickly restored, by the arrest of the soldier, on a charge of stealing glances, and the meeting went on.

"I am appointed Provisional Governor, to secure your forgiveness by means of provisions; and while I would earnestly entreat you, fellow-citizens, never to cease cherishing the glory of that greatest and purest of patriots, Mr. Jefferson Davis, I would also implore you to stand by our noble President in his struggle with the reptiles of the North!"

Captain Munchausen merely turned away for a moment, to make a kick at a Mackerel passing by, and then says he, —

"The sunny South will receive you again as equals! Follow me with your vampyres to my chateau!"

As we followed him, through the shades of evening, I noticed that Captain Villiam Brown was deeply moved.

14*

"Ah!" says Villiam, profoundly, "the sunny South is like the feather-bed of my early years, and grows larger from being well beaten."

And like woman, who is never farther from her conqueror's feet than when she yields to his arms!

Yours, amiably,

ORPHEUS C. KERR.

LETTER XIII.

USHERING IN THE LADY OF THE CHATEAU WITH ALL THE FORMS AND GRACES; INTRODUCING CROQUET AND ONE OF ITS USUAL RESULTS; AND RECORDING THE DIREFUL MISTAKE OF AN UNSUSPECTING UNION OFFICER.

CHIPMUNK COURT HOUSE, May 21, 1868.

How exquisite a creation is woman, as she evokes the soothing melody of home from a seven-octave piano, and warbles the anguish of Italy in a manner to reach the ears of Garibaldi! How like a fairy of patient tenderness and love is she to the little spanklings of the tranquil house, as she fondly confides them to the care of her sweeping mother, while she goes out to do a little shopping; or thoughtfully persuades them from the apartment when one calls whose misery as to what to do with his hat and legs might overtask their delicate young nerves! How softly creak her ministering steps in the sick-room, as she goes every three minutes to see what time it is getting to be, and seldom upsets more than two chairs and the tray of breakfast things on each chronological occasion! How like a soothing vision from some better world is she to her careworn husband, when she acutely sympathizes in all his troubles by having the sick-headache as soon as he commences telling them to her, and ardently shares in all his joys at the exact moment when they take the shape of an invitation to the opera! And then, when adversity comes down upon him to whom she has sworn to send all her bills, and he finds it difficult to buy that daily cheap cigar which he feels compelled as a gentleman to purchase at the gratuitous lunch-saloon where he inexpensively dines, how touching is it to see her so willingly practising all the rigors of economy, — to see her giving only four dollars for a "braid," when she might get one for four and a quarter, and contenting herself with three pounds of "mixed" candies, when French assorted fruit-drops are so much higher!

The arrival of Matilda Munchausen at the chateau of her brother is the event leading me into this train of thoughts; and when I remember how this fair girl freely offered a pair of ear-rings to be melted into cannon for the South, and went with her own feet to carry a pair of embroidered lamp-mats to a sick Confederacy in the hospital, I feel that my eyes, in dying, could not rest upon anything more beautiful and appropriate than a woman's hand presenting me with a crochet smoking-cap.

At the commencement of the recent misunderstanding between the sections, Matilda fled from the chateau to Wilmington, where news of the latest fashions was likely to be soonest heard; and at the period when the prospects of the South seemed darkest, wrote to her brothers that the Elliptic Hoop-skirt was the best. And now, that Reconstruction has set in, and edging is no dearer in Wilmington than it is anywhere else, she has returned hastily to the halls of her fathers to get her back-hair reconstructed.

Captain Villiam Brown and I had just returned from reproving two Mackerels, who had been scalded with hot tea by order of the Provisional Governor for looking at the surrounding country like conquerors, as it were, — we had just returned from this mission of duty, when Matilda Munchausen arrived and asked if anybody had called during the last six years.

"Matilda," said Captain Munchausen, impressively, as he retied the bit of twine which held his vest together in front, "the two blue Vandals before you, trimmed with brass buttons, are — ha! ha! — our Conquerors; and you must not spit on them for the present. Miss Munchausen, Vandals; Vandals, Miss Munchausen."

"Ah!" says Villiam, bowing as one who should look for a pin upon the floor, and recovering himself just in time to save a small black bottle from sliding out of his pocket, "we are Vandals only in our extreme willingness to take a Roam with you."

"And," said I, bowing also, "you are yourself fair enough to make each of us a Cinna."

"Sirs," said Matilda, haughtily, "while you are guests at my brother's chateau, and have your minions on the grass-plat, which is a burning shame, I shall not wear my hair in papers. But you must not bring any of your conquering airs here, and I won't have you looking at my back-hair as if it was anything to be ashamed of because it isn't fixed ex-act-ly like the latest style in New York. Oh!" said Matilda, with energy, "I should like to scratch your eyes out!"

"Matilda! Matilda!" said Captain Munchausen, gloomily.

"Never mind, Sarah," says Villiam, affably, "my fren' and I understand thé fair seck. Ah!" says Villiam, in soft ecstasy, "how like a bounding fawn would that lovely face appear in a new style of spring bonnet which mine eyes beheld of late in Washington! It was," says Villiam, dreamily, "a teaspoonful of lace, seasoned with fine gold-dust, and garnished with raw tummattusses and green ———."

It was a shame that the Provisional Governor interrupted him just then; for her beautiful head was thrown eagerly forward, her eyes were all alight with the radiance of excitement, and her just-parted lips, like a cleft-rose, seemed to exhale the fragrance of sweet thoughts.

"The South, visionary satrap," — said the Provisional Governor, taking off his spectacles to cool them in consequence of his eyes having flashed with indignation, — "the South, visionary satrap, refuses to buy the luxuries of the North, having learned that six months' credit is to be refused with contumely. Now, let us to crockay."

We all followed his lead out doors to the croquet ground, our host having enthusiastically adopted the game, upon information that it was fashionable in Europe, from a cousin who sold lozenges on the Continent. Gaining the spot, and looking down upon the half-hoops sticking into the ground, I was about to speak, when Villiam suddenly gave a start, and I saw Matilda flitting hastily from his side.

"Ah!" says Villiam.

"How now, my Napoleon?" asked I.

"My fren'," says Villiam, in a whisper, "that sweet being pinched me."

"What for?" said I.

"Hum!" says Villiam, rubbing his arm, "methinks she loves me; and she's winkin' at me now."

Alas! for the quick susceptibility of woman's heart! Matilda was indeed winking and motioning in an extraordinary manner just at that instant, and seemed anxious to remind the man of her choice that the terrible fact of their long and secret attachment must on no account be divulged to her brothers. Thus it is that young Love, when first an occupant of woman's nature — bold, yet timid — is ever making an arrow escape!

The mallets with which the game of croquet is played not having arrived from Europe, we were supplied instead with shovels, marked "U. S.;" and as the requisite balls were not found in the barrels from whence the half-hoops were ingeniously extracted, we used apples in their places.

With much chivalry of manner did the dignified Munchausen advance with his shovel and strike an apple through half the hoops, closely followed by Matilda Munchausen, who beckoned Villiam to follow her and struck her apple with still better effect. Villiam, with a heavenly smile upon his countenance, attended to his fruit with equal skill, and the Provisional Governor and I came after in a state of feverish excitement. Wildly raged the manly sport, and all the apples were close together near the last wicket, when there suddenly appeared upon the scene a ravenous pig, of severe visage, who incontinently devoured them in a twinkling of the eye.

"By chivalry!" exclaimed Captain Munchausen, "he's eaten up all the crockay."

"Well, I declare!" said Matilda Munchausen, "to have all spoiled by a pig!"

"Ah!" says Villiam, softly, "be not offended with the accident, sweet warbler. Is not a pig," says Villiam, tenderly, "like a bride, when he plights his troth?"

The noble girl seemed not to hear this beautiful idea; for she looked quickly around to be sure that her brothers were not looking, and then, grasping his nearest hand, she murmured, earnestly, —

"You will not disappoint me?"

"Never!" says Villiam, with dreadful intensity.

She put her face nearer to his, and hissed, —

"Couldn't you put it in a letter?"

"Ah!" says Villiam, beginning to dance ecstatically, "let me put it upon that lovely brow."

"You are kyind, very kyind, sir," whispered the maiden, hurriedly, "but it would not be right to accept such a thing from a stranger."

"Hum!" says Villiam, musingly, "wilt meet me this evening by moonlight alone in the back kitchen?"

"Will you tell me all, then?" she asked, eagerly.

Villiam nodded after the manner of an incorrigible Byron.

"Then I will be there," said Matilda; and flew to regain her brothers who were already walking on.

From that moment, until nightfall, Captain Villiam Brown spake never a word; but I saw that he was steadily growing more depressed, and once or twice I caught him contemplating, with suppressed sighs, a photograph of his mother. Oh, how beautiful is that attribute of our common nature which, at any age, makes our thoughts revert to "Mother" at the approach of a great danger! Even the old man, on the verge of bankruptcy, has been heard to refer respectfully to his mother as one who always cheerfully predicted that he would yet come to want, because, as a boy, he had refused to eat crust; and the young man, whether in a storm at sea, or threatened with marriage, equally regrets having left that mother's side.

As the stars commenced to appear, I walked out with Villiam, and endeavored to calm his natural fears. I told him, that if he felt really unable to purchase one new bonnet, three pairs of balmorals, six lace handkerchiefs and four pairs of gloves per month, it was his duty to avoid making any proposals; but that he must seize her arm the moment she drew a pistol, and trust me to come to his assistance with two muskets from behind the mangle.

"My fren'," says Villiam, with deep emotion, " would

you have me rooflessly destroy all that young being's vision of going to the milliner's and pricing expensive silks all the way down Broadway? No!" says Villiam, sternly, "I will not blight her young life thus, even with silk at its present exciting prices."

Not having it in my heart to protest further against the sweet romance of two fond hearts, I silently armed myself with two muskets from the Mackerel camp on the lawn, and hastened in advance to conceal myself behind the mangle in the back kitchen.

Soon Matilda Munchausen entered by one door, with a lighted candle in her hand, and Villiam came through another with feeble steps.

"Sir," said Matilda Munchausen, "our seneschal, who is just outside the door in the hall, must not be kept waiting too long before locking up the chateau for the night; and so you will please be brief; but, at the same time, I must know all, and I will see if I have enough money."

"Money!" says Villiam, going down upon his knees; "don't think money will buy what I could give thee freely!"

"I am sorry, sir, to find you so intoxicated that you cannot stand on your feet," returned the maiden; "and perhaps you can tell me better at another time."

"Madam," says Villiam, rising with dignity to his feet again, "I had reason to suppose that you were interested in some remarks I made to-day."

"Yes, yes, I was," said Matilda.

A love of a bonnet.

"You asked me to tell you in a letter, and now meet me here on condition of my telling you all?"

"Yes, yes!" ejaculated the now agitated Matilda Munchausen, "and now tell me, how was it trimmed?"

"Ah!" says Villiam, "how was who trimmed?"

Miss Munchausen ate a peppermint drop as she sat on the refrigerator, and says she, —

"Why, the bonnet of course. That bonnet you commenced telling about this morning."

Villiam slapped his left leg with tremendous vehemence, and says he, —

"Come out with the muskets, my fren', and behold the wreck of what was once a man."

As I appeared from behind the mangle, Matilda fled from the kitchen with precipitation, and the seneschal and I stood alone with him.

"Well, my Marshal Ney," said I, pleasantly, "how was it trimmed?"

"With '*Illusion*,' my fren'," says Villiam, sadly; "with '*Illusion*.'"

Better was it thus for him, my boy, than if he had really fallen a matrimonial victim to that strong-minded sex whose occasional manner of resenting breaches of promise seems to indicate, that said promise, as they comprehend it, by anticipation, is promise of breeches.

Yours, indignantly,

ORPHEUS C. KERR.

LETTER XIV.

CHRONICLING THE ARRIVAL OF P. PENRUTHERS AS SUITOR; THE ANCIENT FEUDAL CEREMONIES THEREAT; AND THE DREADFUL DEMEANOR OF THE NOBILITY AT THE ENSUING BANQUET.

CHIPMUNK COURT HOUSE, May 23, 1868.

To the man of limited salary and a religious turn of mind, nothing is more revolting than the presumptuous pride and four-horse turnout of a wealthy person. The man of limited salary and a religious turn of mind, who takes his cheap but happy ride to Central Park in a horse-car, pauses for a moment at the Fifth-Avenue entrance of that park to scratch himself; and, as the sinful vehicles of the rich roll by him, he softly murmurs, "Give me my horse-car and a clear conscience, rather than a basket-phaeton and a soul guilty of wealth. My horse-car may not be inclosed with plate-glass," says he, cheerily, wiping the dust out of his ears; "it may not be devoted to myself alone," says he, scraping the mud from his knees where an Irish-woman's baby had stood upon them during the trip; "but it brings one here as safely as though it were a chariot. Roll on, then, ye hapless children of mammon, in your shining carriages. I ask none of your gold to make me the more virtuous as a man, or the more justly celebrated as an umbrella-maker."

And what, after all, is this wealth, that its possession should bring pride, its loss despair? Its sudden withdrawal in consequence of a Vandal war of emancipation may, indeed, oblige men of imperious natures to go around in straw hats made of the bottoms of baskets, and collars composed of wall-paper; it may compel them to dine and attend church in dressing-gowns made of old window-curtains; but it cannot crush the indomitable souls long accustomed to implicit obedience from persons of African descent; nor humiliate the chivalric minds to which everything from the North, save six months' credit, has always been inexpressibly disgusting.

Imagine yourself here beside me, my boy, at Chipmunk Court House, gazing at the patrimonial chateau of the Munchausens, with four mortgages upon it, and a Dutch-oven sticking out of the side. Has it any less dignity to the sight as the castle of an ancient and knightly race, merely because a temporary misunderstanding with the Rothschilds impels its owner to wear a woollen stocking for a smoking-cap, and a pair of his deceased wife's hose for gloves? Does it loom less princely upon the vision as a stately Southern home, merely because a few of the shingles have fallen from the ramparts, and one of the towers closely resembles a chimney with all the top bricks blown off? You dare not answer in the affirmative. You dare not believe that a temporary misunderstanding with the Rothschilds is any derogation from the native dignity of men who are strangers to fear and a fear to strangers.

On Tuesday morning, while Captain Villiam Brown was shaving himself, in his own room, with the bit of window-glass which our host had lent him for the purpose, and I was seated in my own chamber, upon an old wagon-seat, which served as a sofa, there entered unto me Loyola Munchausen; who, with his usual haughty air, threw himself upon the inverted butter-tub which represented a chair in the suite of Southern cottage furniture.

"I greet your Highness," said I, rising, and pretending a delicate blindness to the fact that the pocket-handkerchief fluttering in his right hand had undoubtedly been manufactured from a discarded night-cap. "I greet your Highness. To what am I indebted for your worshipful company this morning?"

"Sir," said he, loftily, "I can no longer refrain from noticing that you have brought a carpet-bag with you to the South."*

"I cannot deny it," said I, coloring with shame.

"Then, sir," added the imperious Southerner, leaning heavily upon the reversed barrel which served as the toilet-table of the cottage suite, "let me warn you against making that carpet-bag too conspicuous while you remain in the chateau of my knightly brother, Cap-

---

* "Carpet-baggers" is one of the affectionate titles given to Northern visitors by Southern sarcastic journals.

tain Munchausen. The sunny South," says he hotly, "has used no carpet-bags herself since the late Vandal war, and the sight of one in the hands of a Northern Hessian is an insult to her during the present coolness between herself and the Rothschilds."

"Oh," said I, calmly, "I understand you now. The sight of a mudsill carpet-bagger from the Yankee North is an aggravation to the sunny South, because she herself has at present nothing whatever to put into a carpet-bag!"

"Sir," said Loyola Munchausen, rising to his feet again that I might not too closely observe the pair of india-rubbers which he wore as slippers, "you are right. Your military Vandals may have — ha! ha! — conquered the sunny South for a time, and rendered it temporarily difficult for her to pay the interest upon all her mortgages; but she is still too proud to bear the insolence of carpet-baggers in silence."

Pausing for suitable words whereby to confess my own iniquity in possessing any baggage, and my deep sympathy with one of the most sensitive peoples that ever had a trifling difference with the Rothschilds, I was abruptly startled by a tremendous clangor which seemed to come from some point over our heads.

"Dear me!" says I, agitatedly, "is somebody cleaning a brass kettle on the roof; or has the cat got a fit amongst the milk-pans?"

"No, poor Vandal," says Loyola Munchausen, moving

haughtily to the nearest window, and swiftly pulling aside the split coffee-bag which represented its damask curtains; "that is the great bell of the chateau; and it is ringing in honor of the arival of Pendragon Penruthers, Esquire, of Taikachor Court House, who comes in state to sue for the hand of our fair sister, Matilda Munchausen."

The original great bell of the Munchausen chateau, after having called the family to dinner for ages, had been freely melted into cannon during the recent Vandal carnage; but its place was now amply supplied by a large tin dish-pan, in which swung a pewter spoon on a wire; and, as it gave forth its peal of welcome, and I thrust my head through the window to behold the pageant, Captain Villiam Brown's intellectual countenance also appeared from a neighboring casement.

"My fren'," says Villiam, perceptibly trembling, "has a junk-shop exploded anywhere? What is this horrible noise which mine ears behold?"

I told him, in hurried accents, that the great bell was ringing in honor of the Chevalier P. Penruthers, who came from his own baronial halls at Taikachor Court House to demand the hand of Lady Matilda Munchausen in marriage; and when I noticed what a keen expression of pain usurped those particular portions of his countenance where he had cut himself while shaving with the Munchausen family razor, I remembered that he himself had once cast fond eyes upon the heiress. Deeply affected by the thought,

I turned my bit of Smoked Glass to the road below, and there beheld a stately sight.

Mounted upon a spirited snuff-colored barb, whose knee-joints had been finely developed by the equestrian sports of the canal tow-path, was Pendragon Penruthers, Esquire. Attired in white kid gloves, a green bombazine overcoat, red flannel inexpressibles, and a unique, tall, square paper hat, marked "7 lbs. BEST JAVA COFFEE," he recalled to mind all that I have ever read of chivalrous knighthood, and suggested some of the finest knightly portraitures of Sir Walter Scott. At the grand gate, a few slats at the bottom of which had been fractured the night before by the violent entrance of several pigs into the garden, stood that mirror of chivalry, Captain Munchausen, neatly wrapped in his window-curtain.

P. Penruthers wound a shrill blast upon the tin horn which he carried as a bugle, and I regret to say that my friend, Villiam, entirely misconstrued the knightly summons.

"Ah!" says Villiam, "that means fresh fish. Got any porgies?" cries Villiam, in a pleasing voice.

"Hush!" says I, greatly mortified, that is not a fish-horn. He winds his bugle as a summons. Be silent, and mark what follows." Captain Munchausen raised his right hand to the woollen stocking on his head, and says he, —

"Methinks, by our lady, thou blowest a keen blast, Sir Knight. Upon what high embassy comest thou to our ancient chateau?"

Pendragon Penruthers, Esquire, did not dare bow in return, lest the motion should overthrow his steed, which was at that moment standing weakly upon three legs, and trying to scratch himself with the other; but he waved the clothes-pole, which he carried as a lance, and says he, —

"I come, sire, to lay my hand and heart, not to mention mortgages, at the feet of the Lady Matilda Munchausen; and to offer knightly gauge to any losel knight who would say me nay. Give her to me, sire, that my home in the Almshouse may be lonely no more."

"Sir Knight," responded Captain Munchausen, with emotion, "I know you for a member of an old and heavily mortgaged race. Let us break bread together before entering my halls. What, ho, seneschal!"

Here the aged colored seneschal of the chateau made his appearance, bearing a fresh hoe-cake on a dust-pan, and of this the two knights ate in token of amity. At the conclusion of the ceremonial, Captain Munchausen motioned for his noble guest to descend from his fiery charger, and leave the latter leaning up against the fence; and says he, —

"By my halidome, Sir Knight, you will find our ancient grass-plot occupied by a horde of military Vandals from the plebeian North, who are sent to reconstruct us; and the chateau is also defiled by the presence of two Yankee scorpions, who must also be endured for a time."

Mr. Penruthers scowled fiercely, and says he, "Do they bring any capital with them, sire?"

"One of them, at least, has a carpet-bag," returned Captain Munchausen, gloomily.

P. Penruthers laughed a low, blood-curdling laugh, and he hissed through his set teeth, —

"Then I may once more know what it is to wear a clean collar. Let us within."

As they passed in under the massive doorway, which would have been severely Gothic but for the three or four emaciated hens roosting on top of it, I turned to Villiam, and says I, —

"Well, my fellow-scorpion, what think you now of the manners and customs of the superior race?"

Villiam thoughtfully brushed away an excited hen, which was striving to alight upon his head, under the impression that his hair was something to eat, and says he, —

"My fren', if Matilda Munchausen leads that nobleman to the altar, she'll find him the heaviest mortgage you ever heard of." After which malignant expression of disappointed affection, Villiam passionately withdrew from public notice, and resumed his toilet before the bottom of a tin pail which had been placed in his apartment as a mirror.

In about half an hour thereafter, the great bell of the chateau, which had been removed downstairs, rang hideously for dinner; and my friend and I repaired at once to the *salle à manger*, where we were introduced as Vandals to the knight from Taikachor Court House.

Then, having taken seats on the inverted peach-baskets around the sumptuous table, and noticed that the missing leg of the latter had been replaced temporarily by an umbrella, we proceeded to discuss all the latest delicacies of the markets. Pendragon Penruthers, Esq., passed a tin plate marked "U. S." to Villiam, and says he, —

"Sir Vandal, permit me to help thee to some hoecake! and would, by'r lady, it might poison thee!" And, simultaneously, he leaned across the groaning board, and took off my friend's clean collar.

"Hum!" says Villiam, throwing at him a cracker marked "U. S."; "if you do that again, my fren', I shall feel obliged to impeach you in the eye."

"Oh!" says Matilda Munchausen, sticking a fork into me, "how disgusting it is to have Northern reptiles at the same table with one!"

At this crisis, Loyola Munchausen made a pass at Villiam with the wash-hand basin, which served as a bread-tray, and says he, —

"If you can't conduct yourself properly at our wassail-board, Sir Vandal, it will be my painful duty, as a Provisional Governor, to fine you a couple of dollars."

"Ah!" says Villiam, cracking him on the head with the toasting-fork, "we don't wish to alienate the Southern Union element; but if you try to pour anything out of that teapot upon me, my fren', I'll call in my forces."

Here a lamentable outcry came through the windows from the direction of the grass-plot, and says I, —

"What means this?"

"It means, Sir Yankee," says Captain Munchausen, "that I have caused my seneschal to pour some scalding water from the ramparts upon your Vandals out there, in punishment for their having dared to look at our guest like conquerors."

Merely pausing long enough to hurl at him one of the halves of dice-boxes which served us as napkin-rings, Villiam flew from the feast to look after his scalded Mackerels; and I immediately followed him, with one of Matilda Munchausen's potatoes plastered against the back of my head.

My friend was condoling with one of our scorched military Vandals on the lawn, when I reached him, and says I, —

"Are you going back again, Villiam?"

He shook his head sadly, and says he, —

"No, my fren'. It's dangerous for Northern Capital to dine with so many mortgages. Let us wait and take our dinner with the seneschal."

    Yours, in waiting.
        ORPHEUS C. KERR.

LETTER XV.

CITING AN INCIDENT OF THE SOUTHERN POSTAL SERVICE; INTERPOLATING AN IMPEACHMENT NOTE FROM WASHINGTON, AND A VAGUE WORDSWORTHIAN PARODY; AND "CONSERVATIVELY" TOUCHING UPON THE PRESIDENTIAL NOMINATION OF THE LAST MACKEREL GENERAL BY A CLASSICAL CONVENTION.

CHIPMUNK COURT HOUSE, May 28, 1868.

DURING the late violent proceedings of the United States of America against the well known Southern Confederacy, our shameless military Vandals applied the torch of the incendiary to all the fine wooden public buildings of Chipmunk Court House; and I regret to say, my boy, — I mourn to observe, — that they attempted to justify this wanton act, upon the ground that a venerable female Confederacy had indignantly protruded her spectacles from a second-story window while the troops were passing, and hurled a hot rice-pudding at the principal brigadier. Taking advantage of the temporary demoralization produced in the ranks by this dreadful episode, she had also opened a scathing fire of saucepans and flat-irons upon the general army, which so excited the head of the garrison that he at once scraped the pudding out of his whiskers, removed the pudding-dish from his head, and ordered a speedy ignition of the Slave Pen, the Whipping-post and other public edifices. Owing to the fact that the local Fire Department was quite intoxicated at the time, and was advised by his physician to bandage his head with a wet towel before trying to remember where he had left his watering-pot, the flames spread fiercely to the post-office, and destroyed the latter before a single lottery-circular could be got out. Consequently, the present post-office consists of a former apple-stand with a green cotton umbrella spread over it; and thither I repaired from the chateau of the Munchausens, at an early hour this morning, to ask for my mail.

Donning the bottoms of two cologne-water bottles connected by a wire, which served him as spectacles, the aged postmaster searched the blue worsted stocking, which he used as a mail-bag, and says he, —

"'Pears to me I did have a letter to your address; but I don't seem to remember where it is. I haven't shaved lately," says he, meditatively, — "I haven't shaved lately; so I couldn't have used it in that way; and we haven't lit a fire recently; so it can't have been burnt. O—h—h," says he, suddenly brightening up, "I remember now. I let my wife have it last night, to take off the stove-lids with; just wait a minute, until I step to the house and look in the coal-scuttle."

Requesting me to mind the worsted stocking while he was gone, and see that no one rifled the mail, the venerable postal official placed upon his head the scooped rind of a watermelon, serving as his hat, and retired to the large sugar-hogshead which he used as a family villa. Presently, emerging from thence, with a gratified smile upon his countenance, he briskly handed me what I at first took for a crumpled piece of leather, but quickly found to be an envelope, scorched almost to a cinder.

"Upon my word," says I, dispiritedly, "this is a nice-looking letter to get from a friend. It may not have been inspired by 'thoughts that breathe;' but it looks as though it certainly contained 'words that burn.'"

The postmaster came flying out at me with a billet of firewood in his hand, and, says he,—"See here, young man, if you're going to talk sarcastically about the postal branch of the government, I shall have to chastise you for disloyalty. I've tried to make this matter pleasant to you," says he, parentally. "I've tried to get along with you without using passionate language; but you don't seem to know what gratitude means. White paper is very dear just now at the South," says he, explainingly; "and every day, when our oldest families around here want something to wrap a pound of butter in, or to put in the bottom of a cake-pan, or to paste over a broken window, they send to me, and I let them have the letters directed here to men from the Vandal North. Only yesterday," says he, with an injured look, "one of our first ladies came to me for some waste-paper to do up her curls with, and, instead of handing her your letter, I gave her a despatch directed to a military Yankee scorpion named Villiam Brown, Eskevire."

"What!" says I, hotly. "Do you dare to violate private correspondence in this free country?"

He smiled a horrible smile, and says he, —

"Your own Congress, young man, has just decided that an official of the United States of America has a right to do as he pleases with all private correspondence whatsoever; and I shall look into the next letter that comes here for you, to see what you do with all your money. And now," says he, passionately, making a pass at me with the billet of firewood, "if you don't go away, and stop disturbing the business of this office, I'll commit you for contempt of court."

I remembered, then, that our able and investigating Congress had, indeed, asserted the right to examine everybody's private telegraphic despatches, for the purpose of obtaining accurate information as to the family-matters of those members of their theatrical company who, at the last moment, had seceded from Impeachment upon the plea that it was an immoral drama. I realized how unpleasant it must be for some private gentlemen who had telegraphed a profane response to his mother-in-law's seventy-fifth unprepaid lightning request that he would be sure and be careful about her daughter's cold, to have his despatch publicly discussed in legislative halls as having some probable occult bearing upon Impeachment; and I wished that Congress Hadn't!" *

---

* Mr. Butler's Congressional Committee for the investigation of supposed Senatorial corruption in the matter of Impeachment, had claimed the right to seize and use any private telegrams supposably bearing thereon.

Thoughtfully rubbing my head in the place where I had been struck by the billet of firewood, I retreated with great humility to my apartment in the chateau, and there succeeded in extricating my scorched missive from the ashes of its envelope. It was from the Conservative Kentucky Chap, at the Capital, and read thus: "Kentucky has enjoyed herself very much to-day, and will be grossly inebriated this evening. The great Transformation Scene, with which the drama concludes, failed, finally, to work. Don't write or telegraph to any of your female acquaintances for a week; or all your letters and telegrams will be read aloud in Congress, and published in every one of the excellent morning journals, as having aided to corrupt Fessenden and Grimes. Don't send any money to your mother-in-law by mail for a week, or it will be taken out to pay for Impeachment. Weed the nobs and bone the swag."

When a country has become so demoralized, my boy, that a chap of good family and elegant language, like myself, can be familiarly addressed in that way, just as though he were a President and entitled to no respect, it is high time for some sort of change. Not wishing to conceal anything from those members of Congress who have a right to know all about the letters we receive, I may as well observe that "Weed the nobs and bone the swag" means, literally, "Equivocate, like any commercial advertiser, with the nabobs around you, and get them to bet with you." Such counsel I treat with contempt; and, as I am a happy and unmarried man, I have, of course, no mother-in-law to support. As for my letters to female acquaintances, I never penned one that I would not be perfectly willing to have incorporated with the Congressional Impeachment Report; and such ladies as have recently written to me for subscriptions to the "Old Women's Home," or "Lady's Club," are cheerfully referred to that Report for rescripts of such replies as they may otherwise fail to receive.

So, after two postponements and three trials, the Great Transformation Scene has finally failed to work! Seven machinists, at the very last moment, become convinced that the drama is immoral, and refuse to co-operate! Just before the first postponement I saw one of them,

---— a simple soul,
  That lightly draws its pay,
And mileage earns with every limb,
  What should it vote but "Nay"?

I met a little Senate-man;
  He would not be sold, he said;
The air was thick with many a curse
  That clustered round his head.

He had a Western, prairie air,
  And he was wildly clad;
His wink relieved my stony stare; —
  It really made me glad.

"Votes for aquittal, Senate-man,
  How many may you be?" —
"How many? Seven in all," he said,
  And wondering looked at me.

"And where are they? I pray you tell."
 He answered, "Seven are we ;
And some of us to Westward dwell,
 And one in Tennessee.

"Two of us farther Eastward lie,
 In politics twin-brothers ;
And for a mess of pottage, I
 Would vote with them and others."

"You say that some to Westward dwell,
 And one in Tennessee,
Yet ye are seven? — I pray you tell,
 Good man, how this may be."

Then did the Senate-man reply,
 "Seven clearing votes are we;
Two of us from the East and West,
 And one from Tennessee."

"You turn about, my Senate-man,
 Your words my reason rive;
If two are from the loyal States,
 Then ye are only five."

"Their votes are green, as will be seen,"
 The Senate-man replied,
"The board of Chase is their dining-place,
 And they are side by side.

"My eyebrows there I often knit,
 My scruples there I 'Hem!'
And there upon a chair I sit, —
 I sit and talk to them.

"And often after sunset, sir,
 When it is light and fair,
I take my little conscience, too,
 And have it settled there.

"The first that caved was Fessenden,
  Who raised a moaning lay,
Till he released him of his pain
  By speaking half a day.

"So for Acquittal it was said
  His vote was high and dry,
Together round that vote we played,
  My brother Grimes and I.

"And when the ground was safe, you know,
  And we could backward slide,
Fowler and I felt forced to go,
  And there Lie by his side."

"How many are you, then," said I,
  "If two should fail you, even?"
The Senate-man did yet reply,
  "O Mister! we are seven."

"But they have said, those two have said,
  Their votes would not be given?"
'Twas throwing words away: for still
  The Senate-man would have his will,
And said, "Nay, we are seven!"*

Wordsworth? Alas! what are words worth to express one's anguish at the failure of that Great Transformation Scene? Where is the Ben Wade who was to have appeared transfigured in that scene,—elevated to the head of a

---

* The "seven" Republican senators voting "Not Guilty" were: Fessenden, of Maine; Fowler, of Tennessee; Grimes, of Iowa; Henderson, of Missouri; Ross, of Kansas; Trumbull, of Illinois; and Van Winkle, of Western Virginia. Public scandal absurdly accused Chief Justice Chase of swaying two or three votes, during the trial, by the fascinations of his dinner-table; and up to the last moment, Ross and two others were regarded as pledged to Impeachment. — Ed.

redeemed nation, rising like a John Phœnix from his ashes! Were I a Whittier person, I should remark of the Presidency: — Of all the sad words of tongue, or pen, the saddest are these — It might have Ben. But, as it is, I can but sing: Wade down upon the Swanee river, far, far away.

Believing that the above remarks are sufficiently in the school of that ecstatic morning journal, the New York "Times," to render it utterly impossible for the most acute intellect to infer from them anything detrimental to my future political interests, no matter which side may finally win, I hasten back to the commencement of the present week and the fine old Southern family of Munchausen.

At the breakfast-table, on Tuesday morning, Captain Munchausen paused a moment over his hoe-cake, and says he, —

"In honor of our guest, the suitor for our sister's hand, the Chevalier Pendragon Penruthers, I propose that eftsoons we proceed in knightly pageant to that haunt of losel Yankees, where a convention of black-and-tan emancipated terriers will this day nominate a military Vandal for next President of our — ha! ha! — common country."

Penruthers was looking quite gallantly in a black silk basque, lent him by his affianced, a pair of red flannel inexpressibles, and a pair of white kid gloves; and says he, —

"Now, by my halidome, I would not miss the sight, an'

it were even more base-born. Pass me the hoe-cake, thou Yankee varlet."

"Grammercy," says Captain Villiam Brown, after the manner of an ancient nobleman; "an' thou speak to me again in that way, my fren', I'll crack thy costard."

"Pax vobiscum, gentle sirs," quoth Loyola Munchausen. "Let us not quarrel with these Northern churls."

Matilda Munchausen tossed her head so that two hairpins fell into my tin plate, and says she,—

"Oh, that some knight would do a feat of derring-do upon these losel wights, ere they should sit at wassail board with us at all!"

"Matilda! Matilda!" expostulated Captain Munchausen, gloomily, "eat your hoe-cake in silence. It ill becomes our superior race to make our sufferings audible to churlish ears."

Thus in knightly conversation passed the meal, at the conclusion of which the snuff-colored Hambletonian of P. Penruthers, Esquire, was hitched with trunk straps to the family carriage, marked "U. S. Ambulance;" and we all rode merrily to the building in which the Convention was being held. Owing to the high price of brown stone and white marble, just now, in the sunny South, this imposing edifice had been rapidly constructed of fence-rails and condemned horse blankets. Its order of architecture was what might be technically termed the no-Capital Corinthian; and over the entrance waved a national flag which gave evidence of having been economically fabricated from a torn sheet, a red flannel shirt, and a pair of blue overalls. Soap-boxes had been placed on end in the interior for the accommodation of delegates and visitors; and upon these we seated ourselves just as the Chaplain arose to preface the vote with a devout petition.

The good man prayed that all persons there assembled, whatever their hue and cry, might be brought to vote as they had been told to, and to give up all their bad habits and —

Here the Hon. GEORGE WASHINGTON arose to a point of privilege; but was taken down again.

The Chaplain went on to express the hope that these delegates, and all other delegates whatsoever, might be taught to distrust their own wisdom, and to cease that excessive drinking which —

Hon. TIBERIUS CÆSAR here moved the previous question, and was at once obliged to move it back again.

Instead of proceeding with his devotions, the Chaplain now complained that the Hon. CAIUS GRACCHUS was "making eyes at him." Even as he spoke, a putty-ball, thrown by the Hon. NUMA POMPILLIUS, smote him on the nose; whereupon he descended from his soap-box in great agitation and promptly engaged the latter delegate in single combat.

These preliminaries being settled, it was then proposed that the Last General of the Mackerel Brigade be nominated by acclamation, and that a Platform be built for him. Both of which propositions were successful.

Yes, sir, both were enthusiastically indorsed; and if you expect me to say any more on the subject just now, you are doomed to disappointment. Throughout this whole letter I have displayed great political ability, and marvellous purity of motive, in endeavoring to walk on both sides of the way at once. To say another word about the above enthusiastic nomination on this occasion, would be to commit myself one way or the other; and I must peremptorily decline so doing. A splendid-looking, gloriously gifted, pure-minded young man is dependent upon me for support, and I must not risk his interests by too hastily taking sides. He, himself, richly deserves to be President, and his name is

Entre nous,
ORPHEUS C. KERR.

LETTER XVI.

SHOWING HOW A DISLOYAL TELEGRAPH DID PERVERT AND MISPUNCTUATE THE MACKEREL GENERAL'S "LETTER OF ACCEPTANCE;" AND SPIRITEDLY DEPICTING THE GREAT MUNCHAUSEN HUNT AND ITS LAMENTABLE ENDING.

CHIPMUNK COURT HOUSE, June 4, 1868.

IN consequence of a temporary financial misunderstanding, superinduced by the not remote military outrages of Federal Vandals upon a knightly people, and still prevailing with great fervor in this sunny clime, the telegraphic facilities here lack that complete typographical finish which is observable in the higher electric circles of wealthy monetary centres. The "First National Bullion Bank" of this place, in the temporary dearth of gold, has a reserved Specie Fund of some two grosses of brass buttons; which have coated at a fabulous premium ever since the spring month known in Southern almanacs as Sherman's MARCH, and still fluctuate wildly as news of Congressional proceedings indicate that the high-strung nobility of this section are, or are not, to wear cotton dressing-gowns forever. In order, then, to obtain prompt intelligence from our distracted National Capital, and so regulate its rates in accordance with the variations of the Impeachment pageant, the "First National Bullion Bank" recently encouraged the formation of a joint-stock company for the construction of a telegraph to the nearest station. Ten capitalists in dressing-gowns at once responded with venerable garden-rakes, which were ably erected along the roadsides at proper intervals, as the poles of the new enterprise; other daring speculators contributed numerous yards of old bell-wire, which was pieced out with sections of hoopskirt-springs and laid carefully across the tops of the rakes, and a battery, composed of two pickle-bottles, an oyster-can, two bent stair-rods and half a pound of blue vitriol, was placed in the hen-house selected as the office of the company.

It is a slight drawback to the pleasures of familiar intercourse with this bloated monopoly that its President reserves the right to read and make literary improvements in all despatches addressed to Northern men; and that he is very apt to send his love at the bottoms of your telegrams to female acquaintances; but the enterprise will yet be self-sustaining, if a wholesome check can be placed upon those members of the freed-negro race who have a present habit of stealing the rakes at night; and with the completion of Reconstruction we shall witness the establishment of an efficient police, to prevent the roosting of fowls along the line.

We have found such cool knights down here, that Captain Villiam Brown has taken cold, and is obliged to keep constantly with him an oblong tin medicine-chest, containing the cough-syrup known to the poets as "red eye." While he and I were allaying our pulmonary injuries with this night-blooming balsam, in my chamber at the Munchausen chateau, on Wednesday, a messenger burst furiously in upon us with a telegraphic despatch; which, on examination, I found to be the Response of the Last General of the Mackerel Brigade to his nomination for President of the United States in 1869.

"Huzza, my Chief-of-Garrison!" says I, patriotically; "just listen to this able document." Whereupon I took out my piece of Smoked Glass — to save my eyes from over-dazzling — and read from the bottom of a bandbox, on which the Telegraph Company had inscribed it, the following

LETTER OF ACCEPTANCE.

"If elected to the office of President of the United States, it will be my end ever to aid many steer all the laws.

"In good faith, to live with economy and with the view of having peace, quiet, and protection anywhere in times like the present, it is impossible, or at least eminently improper, to lay down.— A policy to be adhered to, right or wrong, through an administration of four years.

"New political issues are constantly arising the view of the public on; Old Ones are constantly changing, and a public Administrator should always be sleep-free to execute the wills of the people. I have always respected that —(will, and always shall!) peace and, in reversal, posterity. Its sequence, with economy of Administration, will lighten the burden.

"Of taxation, while it constantly induces the national death, let us have a piece.

"(Blue Seal.)   GENERAL MACKEREL BRIGADE."

"Ah!" says Villiam, wildly clawing the air, like one in great vertigo.

My own brain was spinning in a revolutionary manner; but I strove to be calm, and says I, —

"It appears to me, Villiam, that this great document is worthy of Carlyle. As I understand it, the writer simply pledges himself not to 'lay down;' and seems to imagine that it is a chief part of a President's duty to administer upon wills."

"My fren'," says Villiam, cautiously taking the bottom of the bandbox, to read therefrom for himself, "if some of this here able essay hasn't been lost on the way, through being drawn off by chickens roosting on the wires, it's my opinion that this is the most peaceful and non-committal epistle that ever exploded on the naked ear."

After which remark Villiam and I conversed in whispers upon the great metaphysical subject, until an accurate Republican morning journal reached us from the North, and we found therein the following

CORRECT VERSION.*

"If elected to the office of President of the United

---

* It seemed too bad to pervert General Grant's frank and soldierly Letter, but the temptation was irresistible.

States, it will be my endeavor to administer all the laws in good faith, with economy, and with the view of giving peace, quiet, and protection everywhere. In times like the present it is impossible, or at least eminently improper, to lay down a policy to be adhered to, right or wrong, through an administration of four years. New political issues, not foreseen, are constantly arising; the views of the public on old ones are constantly changing, and a purely administrative officer should always be left free to execute the will of the people. I always have respected that will, and always shall. Peace and universal prosperity — its sequence — with economy of administration, will lighten the burden of taxation, while it constantly reduces the national debt. Let us have peace."

I looked at Villiam questioningly, and says I, —

"In the present depressed state of affairs, my Mars' own child, the Southern telegraph would appear to be eccentric in punctuation, and disloyal in typography. Allow me to taste a little more of your cough-syrup."

"No, my fren'," says Villiam, hastily putting aside his medicine-chest. "After such rebel trifling with my feelings, 'the red eye of bottle is shut in despair.'"

We might have discussed the question further, but for an extraordinary noise coming up from below our window, outside, causing us to look hastily forth from the casement. And there, in the court-yard of the chateaü, with his head thrown slightly back, his right knee thrown a trifle forward, to support his instrument, and his corresponding hand laboriously turning the crank, was a scion of one of the First Families that ever saw better days. His coat was the waist of a calico frock, which had not been warranted to wash; his inexpressibles were the former sleeves of another frock; his hand-organ was a coffee-mill inclosed in a candle-box; and attached to a string, grasped by his left hand, was a small black child to represent a monkey.

"Behold," says I to Villiam, "how greatly reduced in circumstances are this once opulent and chivalrous people, when one of them is thus compelled to organize for a living."

"Ah!" says Villiam, sceptically, "I saw a more reduced objeck than he, yesterday, my fren'. It was a New York pickpocket," says Villiam, confidentially, "who had come down here on speculation; and in twenty-seven Southern wallets—which had once, my fren', been used as infants' shoes—he had found only four buttons and a seidlitz powder. He took the latter," says Villiam, gloomily.

Ay, my countrymen, the man was dead-broke.

Dead-broke, Mr. President. Dead-broke, my Senators and Congressmen. Dead-broke, Right Reverends and wrong Reverends of every order. Dead-broke, men and women, born with heavenly compassion in your hearts. And prying thus around us every day!

But, alas! even while the despairing poor are endeavoring to smother their misery with the deadly seidlitz powder, the aristocratic and gay go on with their giddy sports, as though the world knew no keener sorrow than the soiling of a white waistcoat. From our meditation upon the woes of others, my friend and I were called forth to the field by the aged colored seneschal of the chateau, to join a brilliant cavalcade of lords and ladies in the Munchausen Hunt.

This regular Southern Spring Meeting took particular eclat from the rumor that a fox had escaped from a menagerie, recently travelling through the place on its road to bankruptcy; and as the animal must have been at large on the surrounding estates for nearly a week, and could not live upon mortgages, it was argued that his near approach to death by starvation would render it nearly possibly for the thoroughbred hunters and hounds of the Munchausens to keep up with him.

At any rate, upon arriving at the site of an ancient cabbage-patch, we found the assembled party in great spirits. Sir Pendragon Penruthers, mounted gallantly upon his own snuff-colored blooded racer, cut quite a figure in his black silk basque; and as Villiam had recovered his clean collar from him, in the course of a single combat near the refrigerator on the preceding evening, he now appeared in a standing-collar, cravat, and pair of gloves, done in white paint. Captain Munchausen, in his dressing-gown, occupied a thoroughbred mare, which I took to be a cross between a Hambletonian and a skeleton-wagon, the springs and axles being clearly defined under the sagacious animal's glossy coat. Loyola Munchausen, in his surtout of patent-striped Water-Proof Awning, hat made of half a boot-leg, and top-boots manufactured from sections of stove-pipe, bestrode a prancing bay, which was shaped not unlike a narrow kitchen-table with the leaves down and a pig's head on one end. Matilda Munchausen appeared upon a sorrel palfrey, whose marked fluted developments on either side seemed to indicate that the spirited creature might be opened and shut like an accordion. Matilda wore a riding-skirt of organdy,—supposing organdy to be extensively used this season to imitate one bombazine petticoat sewed to the bottom of another,—and her jaunty jocky-cap of muskmelon rind, and honiton veil of mosquito-netting, reminded me of Sir Walter Scott's Diana Vernon. The two stately gray pacers assigned to Villiam and myself had rather too much trestle-work about them to be comfortable as steeds, however well suited they might have seemed to civil engineers as studies for suspension bridges; but, as they exactly resembled the other hunters in having the trade-marks "U. S." on their flanks, I could not doubt that they came of the same fiery breed. The Munchausen Huntsman, who was a member of the freed-negro race, stood just beyond us, poker in hand, to restrain the energy of the panting hounds,—a majority of which must have looked well when trotting under their native butcher-carts, but now wore a melancholy air of having decided in their own minds that such a thing as a butcher must have been merely a feverish dream of the past. In fact, the whole scene was more English than American; and when the pack was set loose in full cry, fires of chips kindled under all our hunters by the seneschal to make them start, and the shout of "Tally-ho!" sounded by P. Penruthers, saluted my ears, I felt like a British nobleman.

Away we flew like the wind, — supposing the wind to zigzag and come down upon its knees, occasionally, by reason of a little touch of spavin. Tally-ho! Tally-ho! and along we hopped in frantic chase; only now and then stumbling over such of the dogs as had suddenly paused in mid-career to take nervous nips along their backbones. Tally-ho! Tally-ho! and wildly we scudded over the Hampton plantation, leaping mortgages after mortgages, and dauntlessly putting our good steeds at the very deepest sheriff's levies. Just after running against a haystack, Pendragon Penruthers allowed Villiam and myself to come alongside; and says he, —

"By'r lady, and I win not the brush this day, call me losel Yankee churl!"

"Pardie!" panted Villiam, from half-way up the neck of his charger, "an' thou reflect upon me again, my fren', I'll whack thy halidome."

Tally-ho-ahoe! — and we could see the hounds all tangled together in a standing snarl, the older ones making a dead "point" at something in the grass. But we found the latter to be only a dried bone which had been dropped there in olden times by our military Vandals; and on we all flew again, with the first mortgage on the Peyton estate just in sight.

Munchausen Hunt

Tally-ho! Tally-ho!—Captain Munchausen's dressing-gown standing out from his waist like some monster ruffle, Loyola's Water-Proof Awning fluttering high behind his shoulders after the manner of dragon's wings, P. Penruther's black silk basque catching the wind in the likeness of a complicated balloon, and Matilda's long skirt giving her the aspect of a giant umbrella tied to a flying mastodon.

At the very height of this awful excitement, and while I was anxiously scanning the fields ahead through my piece of Smoked Glass, a yellow animal suddenly started out from the bushes just beyond the hounds, and, after tapping one of the latter slightly upon the nose, scudded frantically away toward an adjacent chateau, with tail erect and greatly magnified.

Simultaneously, the maddening "view-halloo!" was given by somebody, and in two more seconds Villiam and I, crying "Yoicks-yoicks!" had thrown ourselves from our foundered hunters under the very walls of the chateau. The fox had entered an opening in the stone foundation of the edifice, and passed under the ancient building; and around the hole sat all the dogs on their hams, in magisterial semicircle, with their tongues hanging waggishly out of their mouths.

Feverishly eager to secure poor Reynard's brush before the others could arrive, Captain Villiam Brown promptly knelt before the hole, and, peering therein, beheld two luminous green glass balls, of the size of the marbles of his childhood. Then, thrusting his right arm far in under the chateau, a sound was heard as of an irascible elderly gentleman spitting from a casement, and my friend changed countenance and hastily drew out his arm again.

"Ah!" says Villiam, excitedly, "as sure as you live, my fren', the fox has gone and scratched me."

In the moment, and while yet he was unguardedly stooping almost double, a window right at my nose flew open like magic, an aged unmarried sister-in-law of the late Southern Confederacy appeared thereat, armed with a huge butter-paddle, and passionately used the latter to inflict an ear-splitting spank upon the absorbed fox-hunter.

Overcome by feelings too intense to be expressed in print, the nearly murdered Federal officer leaped high into the atmosphere, and came down upon a dog that was making his toilet.

"Ah!" says Villiam, rubbing himself, "what made you do that to me, Miss Southerland?"

The venerable maiden made a pass at me, also, with the still quivering butter-paddle; and says she,—

"If I catch you chasing after my innocent cat in that way again, young man, I'll hurt you wuss'n that!"

Here the other members of the hunt came tottering up to the chateau, to apologize to Miss Southerland for our ill-bred Yankee mistake; and, as the sight of two distant Northerners, in straw hats, had rendered our horses too restive for mouthfuls of the latter to make further hard riding safe, it was agreed that we should all return home forthwith.

It being evident that the sufferings of the wounded Federal officer would be increased by additional saddle-exercise, he preferred to walk, and I with him; nor could I disguise my admiration at the manner in which this heroic young man drew a useful moral from his late disaster.

"My fren'," says he, limping slightly, "more than once has he who would catch the Fox with one tail, come nearer catching the Cat of nine tails."

Yours, credulously,
Orpheus C. Kerr.

LETTER XVII.

ILLUSTRATING THE TREMENDOUS EXTRANEOUS INFLUENCE OF LARGE-SIZED NAMES; AND DESCRIBING THE MOST PASSIONATE AND CONTEMPTUOUS LOVE-SCENE EVER BEHELD IN FASHIONABLE SOUTHERN SOCIETY BY A YANKEE VARLET.

CHIPMUNK COURT HOUSE, June 12, 1863.

A NOSE by any other name would smell as sweet, my boy, — which may account for the occasional use of the term "bugle" in that connection; but who can doubt that the proper name of a man may sometimes give him a popular sweetness quite beyond the attainment of mere virtue or genius? Why is it that we so instinctively realize our own insignificance, and feel crushed with a vague and awful reverence, when confronted with such names as Paracelsus, Cagliostro, and Theodore Tilton? Then, again, how is it that, by writing out all the names they have, on every possible occasion, some men may attain an inexpressible eminence, which had never been so amply accorded to their mere patronymics alone? Look at Ralph Waldo Emerson, James Russell Lowell, Oliver Wendell Holmes, and Martin Farquhar Tupper. There is something LARGE-SIZED about names in this style; something swelling and tremendous; and they virtually make a pass at you with a big club, and say: "There is much in the very sound of us that is more high-toned than language can express, and if you will now prostrate yourself in the dust before us, without further confusion, we will sit down upon you for a while on this pleasant summer day." You say to yourself that you have your best clothes on, that the dust is disagreeable, and that your feeble intellect fails to discover any reason just now why you should be so crushed; but down you go, and are sat upon.

Reconnoitring the political field, after the manner of a practical philosopher, and realizing that Ulysses is the first name of one Presidential aspirant, and Pendleton the family-name of another, I am at once overpowered with intimidating classical memories of the amazing single combat with bully Ajax for the armor of Achilles, and almost suffocated with depressing premonitions of immense shirt-collar, gold-headed cane, and other pharaphernalia of deep-voiced Respectability. In the mere sound of Ulysses I hear the assertion: "There are several collegiate Greek reasons why I should take a little walk over you for my health, whether you can find any English reasons for the same or not." And in the sonorous roll of Pendleton I recognize the sentence: "If you come of good family, young man, and have a letter of recommendation from your father, you may tell your friends that I have noticed you."

When, upon a late occasion, I took up a copy of the "Daily Mortgage," — a loyal journal, published here every morning on bits of old muslin, — and remarked the popular enthusiasm with which the Presidential nomination of

Ulysses, last General of the Mackerel Brigade, has been received, I could not help feeling that a crushing name is half the battle. In one column I found a letter to the name from an influential gentleman in South Carolina, who wrote: "All hail, sir! I take this opportunity to pledge the State of New Hampshire for a majority of at least fifteen thousand votes in your favor; and if you could make it convenient to lend about three dollars and a half to a man who has always respected you, the prompt remittance of that amount to my address would greatly oblige me." Another gentleman of high position, at Mugby Six-Forks, Florida, writes: "The Empire State of New York will respond to your nomination in a tone of thunder; and should you see fit to notice the enclosed card of the Mugby State Lottery, the immediate mailing of one dollar will entitle you to a large farm in Alaska, less our commissions." A venerable leader of society in Bowieville, Arkansas, says: "Greetings, illustrious Soldier! Next November will find the good old State of Connecticut standing shoulder to shoulder with her sister States in the triumph of your cause; and by enclosing four shillings to the address here given you will receive my 'Advice to Those About to Marry,' by return of mail."

Turning to the editorial page of this same journal, — the editor of which makes quite a good living and almost pays the interest of his mortgages by alternately writing articles in his office and selling ginger-snaps on the trains, — I find a tribute to the other name. "Mr. Pendleton," says the editorial, "is a dignified gentleman, of enviable social Position and refined Antecedents; nor do the most elegant annals of distinguished Society present the old family-name of one taking higher rank in the walks of unblemished respectability. His position in Circles to which we all look for models of high-bred gentility is unassailed by the remotest suspicion of plebeian Extraction; while his polished Manners and courtly Address will ever commend him to the most exclusive Appreciation in this community, where our well-known fellow-citizen Wade Hampton Breckenridge, Esq., is now offering a large stock of ably selected family groceries at prices which few would credit, and for which he gives no credit himself."

Just sound over these names to yourself, my boy, and see how they will make you grovel, whether you want to or not. Then ask yourself whether a John Jobkins or a James Podgers could ever attain so much world-wide reverence by any great act he might accomplish? See what your own noiseless name has done for you! You think yourself handsome (poor wretch!), and believe that you are both Great and Good; but you have not yet succeeded in gaining even the respect of your mother-in-law. No, sir! no one has any respect for you; and unless you induce the Legislature to change your name to something like Aurelius Stanhope Jinks, I don't see how you are going to keep out of the Poor-house this summer.

Why, look at me, here, in this great Southern monetary centre, being crushed out of all self-respect and self-defence by the name of Pendragon Penruthers, Esquire. This knight does not wear such clothes as one would like to see George Washington dressed in; yet he has so cowed me by his mere nominal sound, that I am growing more and more self-depreciatory in his presence; and a subtle intuition of this fact makes him actually ignore my low Yankee existence on occasions.

This morning, while I sat quietly upon a butter-firkin, which had been sawed into an easy-chair, in the drawing-room of the ancient Munchausen chateau, P. Penruthers entered, with Matilda Munchausen hanging upon his arm, and escorted her to a wash-bench, which had been covered with a rag-carpet to represent a luxurious settee. Then, drawing over his hands a pair of white cotton socks, which he had borrowed from Loyola for courting-gloves, and displaying them in a manner to impress her with his splendors of costume, he buttoned his silk basque to his neck to make himself emotionally hoarse, and says he, —

"Miss Munchausen, further concealment of my feelings were useless; by 'r lady, I love — "

Here I coughed to remind them of my presence; whereupon he waved one of the socks toward me, in a haughty manner, and says he, —

"You see, fayre lady, that NOBODY is here."

Matilda ate a slate-pencil dipped in vinegar to keep herself from growing stout, and says she, —

"Yes, my Lord, I see that yonder easy-chair is VACANT."

The faintly scornful sound of these casual remarks stung me into a conciousness that I was indeed a Nobody, and presented a marked aspect of Vacancy; but, even with the misfortunes of my Vandal Northern birth and noiseless name, I have moments of vague self-respect; and, with an air of considerable hauteur, I drew out my piece of Smoked Glass and proceeded to gaze thoughtfully through it at the pageant of Love's Young Dream.

"Matilda," went on Pendragon Penruthers, in a deep base voice, "our Families are equally Old; ancient mortgages draw us together, and it becomes us to complete the holy tie. Hessian Vandals from the scorpion North are buying up our fair domains at about seven dollars per castle and private park, and I expect, by my halidome! to realize some thirteen dollars and a quarter for mine own estate withal. With this amount, I can safely run in debt for one year, and I ask you, ladie fayre, to help me therein."

"My heart's Pendragon Penruthers," sighed Matilda, drawing off a blue worsted mitten and giving him one of her hands to kiss. "I am but a poor weak maiden, unaccustomed to public speaking, and have but onethird-mortgage in mine own right. If that is any inducement, you might take me; but first, let me ask, are you a Ritualist?"

P. Penruthers smote his forehead with one of his socks, then seized a hymn-book lying upon a Louis

Seize table (flour-barrel covered with drugget) near at hand, and tore it into thirty-one fragments.

"Matilda," says he, frenziedly, "I cannot tell a lie. A clergyman living next to me once had one of his cherry-trees cut down, and I did it with my little hatchet. I am an infidel, a pagan, and a spiritualist. Let me not hide such facts from thee, dear one, — now that NOBODY is listening."

She threw up her white arms, and he, expecting a blow from her, drew hurriedly back and pitched headlong over the sand-box, which (as he chewed) he had taken care to have near his feet before beginning the conversation. She had meant nothing, however, but the most trustful affection; and, as the arrogant knight slowly picked himself up from the floor and made a stealthy reach for the poker, the lady of the chateau, by a sudden movement, caught his head under one of her arms, and spat a loud kiss upon his forehead.

"And think you, my dearest lord," cried she, "that I would turn from you on that account? No! You have said that you cannot tell a lie, and you did it with your little hatchet. Could a George Washington do more?"

"Do I remind you of Washington, then?" asked P. Penruthers, softly, wriggling his head out of chancery, and regaining his feet again.

"Very much," she murmured.

An expression of melancholy settled upon his countenance, and he folded his socks over the breast of his silk basque.

"Matilda," said he, huskily, "is the interest on your mortgage all paid up?"

"Yes, Pendragon."

Again the anguished knight smote his forehead with a sock, and says he, "How can I tell this trustful being the whole truth? How can I reveal to her that my present home is in — the Almshouse!"

She darted out her fair hands toward him; and he, anticipating a blow after such a revelation, attempted to withdraw a pace, and tripped heavily over my feet. But her gesture had meant only a demonstration of augmented attachment, and, before he could arise from the ground, she flew at him, took his face between her mittens, and smiled down at him.

"Pendragon Penruthers," she said, very distinctly, "just lie where you are, and listen to me. Rather would I give Matilda's hand, heart, and mortgage to you, a Southerner, though in the Almshouse, than to a Northerner with the carpet-bag of a Crœsus."

His position being unfavorable for any other gesture of pleasure, Mr. Penruthers kicked ecstatically in the air with those limbs, on which appeared his red flannel inexpressibles, and says he, —

"Then, by my halidome, I ask no more. Thou art mine, Matilda; and; come weal or woe, we will starve together."

"And allow me," said I, putting up my Smoked Glass, "to congratulate you on the spot."

At the disagreeable Northern sound of my voice, the lady of the chateau permitted the fallen nobleman to reach a standing position once more, and he cast a supercilious glance toward my easy-chair.

"I see NOBODY," says he, contemptuously; "and yet I heard a hideous noise."

Matilda tossed her head, and says she, "I heard NOBODY speak."

"So did I," quoth Pendragon Penruthers, Esquire.

After which they both looked directly at me for five minutes, in the manner of those who would have their nearest personal friends understand that they are staring at vacancy, and then retired from the apartment with great aristocracy of demeanor.

Had plain John Smith treated me thus, do you think, my boy, that I would have borne it? No, sir! I should have gone after John on one foot, and attempted, for a single energetic instant, to climb his backbone with the other. But a man named Pendragon Penruthers, Esquire, *must*, in some way, have a right to exhibit a far greater immensity of aspect than one who is only

Yours, unassumingly,

ORPHEUS C. KERR.

LETTER XVIII.

CASUALLY EXPLAINING THE UNIQUE LATIN MOTTO OF AN ANCIENT HOUSE; BUT CHIEFLY DEVOTED TO A BRILLIANT CHIVALRIC TOURNAMENT, AND SHOWING HOW THE NOBILITY AND GENTRY DEMEANED THEMSELVES ON THAT KNIGHTLY OCCASION.

CHIPMUNK COURT HOUSE, June 15, 1868.

IT is only in the South, that our distracted Republic possesses any of that dignity of ancestry and pride of castellated outbuildings, which are familiarly described by those more celebrated American travellers who have been admitted to the principal kitchens of Europe. Here, as I sit musing before the grand old chateau of Captain Munchausen, with the Conic Section of the Mackerel Brigade encampment upon the lawn beyond me, and at my right, the Provisional Governor, on a barrel, trying four members of the freed-negro race for refusing to work for four dollars and a half a year, — as I sit thus surrounded by all the exciting richness of a land's affecting redemption from error, methinks I can see far back into the antiquity of this chivalric people, and hold spiritual converse with the grand old cavaliers. Methinks I see the celebrated and high-spirited Duke of Lee, in his rich corduroy mantle and Vandyke hat with turnpike tickets in the band, guiding the blooded steeds of his chariotful of early cabbages to market. Methinks I behold the Earl of Hunter, attired in the rim of a straw hat and robes slashed with white under-clothing, bending pensively over the sweet-potato patch and reckoning the probable profit on his jewelled fingers. Methinks I observe the brilliant Marquis of Pendleton, in his plumed helmet of ventilated white beaver and toga of alpaca, making boots and shoes for the nobility and gentry of the castles adjoining his own.

Then, as I look up at the patrimonial chateau of Munchausen, with four mortgages upon it, and a Dutch oven sticking out of the side, I at once feel that there is an unspeakable lowness about everything but hunting, and experience an inordinate desire to be supported by a colored man.

Taking the arm of Captain Villiam Brown, who had just been shaving himself with a bit of glass sent to his room for that purpose, and following the direction of the aged seneschal who was carrying in the hoe-cake on a dustpan, I proceeded to the *salle à manger*, where Captain Munchausen, Matilda, P. Penruthers, and the Provisional Governor were awaiting us. Each being pointed to his proper inverted peach-basket by the master of the revel, we seated ourselves thereon around the groaning board.

Wishing to promote conversation, I helped myself to some hard-tack, and said I, —

"Tell me, my mirror of knighthood, what mean these letters ' U. S.,' which I find imprinted upon the crackers, the tomato can, the claret cork, upon every eatable on this wassail board, except the hoe-cake?"

Captain Munchausen drew closer around his shoulders the calico window-curtain which formed his *robe de chambre*, and says he, —

"By Chivalry! they mean ' *Unum Semper*,' or 'One Always,' which is the Latin motto of my family."

"Ah!" says Villiam, dreamily, "give us this day our daily Unum Semper. Do you know, my fren'," says Villiam, pleasantly, "that all the meals of our Mackerel beings are Unum Sempers too?"

"Sir Vandal," said Captain Munchausen, "your remarks must not be tolerated. Will you have a clean knife and fork?"

"Yes, sarah," says Villiam, majestically, "and another spoonful of motto, if you please."

"Seneschal," said Captain Munchausen, "go to the armory and bring some more knives and forks."

"Stop, brother," said the Provisional Governor, observing that our haughty host was making movements as though to stab Villiam in the back with a butter-knife; "this is no time for the South to bluster. Let us rather stand by our noble President in his conflict with the scorpions of the North."

"Sir," responded the proud Virginian, "you teach me my jooty. And now what say you?—shall we invite the vipers to our tournamong, that they may witness the ancient knightly pastime of the superior race whom they have — ha! ha! — conquered?"

Here Captain Munchausen laughed horridly; and would

have grown hysterical with scorn had he not suddenly remembered that his knees, which he had drawn up to the rim of the wassail-board, were looking forth like a couple of bald-headed prisoners through the airy interstices of their respective sable dungeons. Whereupon he arose quickly to his feet, and says he, "Seneschal, how stands our ancestral treasury?"

The aged servitor stopped cleaning the knives, and says he, —

"S' help me gad, Mars'r, I hab done got only two shillings for workin' de whole day yerserday for one of dem Yankees down yar."

A terrible smile trickled over those of Captain Munchausen's features which illuminated his whiskers like lamps in a forest, and says he, —

"Will the Messieurs Vandal be good enough to note the — ha! ha! — blessing of Freedom to the colored race? Will they note how the freedman is able to support himself? Two shillings a day!! Seneschal," said Captain Munchausen, hastily, "give me the two shillings, then, and I will to try to get along with them."

The venerable retainer passed the largesse to his lord, and soon we all started for the field of chivalric adventure, after the manner of several Ivanhoes.

Now, spirit of Orlando, thou matchless paladin and sturdy hater of cold water in any application, come to my aid with as much brass helmet as possible, while I describe the scene of Arturian splendor which exploded upon our vision when we reached the field of tournay.

A piece of historical ground, which had proved upon trial to be unfavorable to potatoes, had been set apart for the knightly pageant; and all four sides of it were supplied with an ancient staging of four descending seats, which ended at short intervals in pillars driven into the ground. A lavish baron of the olden time, who did quite a good thing in the oyster trade, had bequeathed the interest of seven dollars per annum as a fund for keeping the staging impregnable to vagrant cows, and the fact that only a few roasting pigs were grazing in the lists, when we arrived, spoke well for the use of the legacy.

The top seat all around, singularly narrow as it was, seemed to have the preference; and, as its occupants were privileged to hook their insteps and ankles on the next seat below, and the two seats still lower were chiefly practicable for the use of chickens, I did not wonder at the choice.

Captain Villiam Brown and I now took out the bits of Smoked Glass with which we always protect our eyes when viewing dazzling spectacles, and surveyed the knights and ladies as they arrived and climbed to the top seat.

"Ah!" says Villiam, "if that rail should happen to turn, my fren', how many would experience reverses!"

We were both of us cogitating over this idea, when Captain Munchausen motioned for us to take seats on the barrels next to his, and says he, —

"Hist, Hessians! see you not, by 'r lady, that the contending knights have arrived?"

Sure enough, my boy, two or three of the seats had been let down upon the other side of the glittering arena, and there entered four stately figures upon steeds branded with the motto, "U. S." Forward they came across the field, to pay their devoirs to the Queen of Love and Beauty in a bonnet of the latest fashion of the Spring of '61; while a party of New York heralds erected, at proper points in the lists, posts from whose cross-bars hung many curtain rings.

First of the champions was Sir Cooke de Puddingwell, in a casque of soft black felt, through the top of which some locks of his hair protruded in an ingenious plume. His colors were crimson, and he wore them in the shape of a red flannel under-garment which flowed upon his breast between the flaps of his rather-tight-at-the-waist alpaca mantle.

Next was the Viscount Morgeejee, descended from a noble Welsh family of cavaliers, in a *chapeau de straw*, shaped somewhat like an umbrella, and a dress-coat of rich cotton velvet, gored and made low in the neck. His colors were blue merino, and he wore them in quatriform patches on each knee.

Thirdly was Sir Blessingen Desguys, of French cavalier stock, in a helmet of black silk with very little of the nap rubbed off, and a mantle of brown linen trimmed with tulle and hem-stitched up the front with narrow edging on

the sleeves, and gored down the back, with a frill of applique at the waist. His colors were a yellow silk handkerchief, one end of which protruded behind his ear from under his helmet.

The last was Sir Render Awdye, in a white plush helm, which he was reported to wear in bed, a rich jacket of green baize with round bone blazonries, and the quarterings of his coat-of-arms engrossed upon his costume just below the brief tails of his jacket. He appeared to have no colors, being only a banneret; but something white occasionally appearing at the foot of his spine as he moved in the saddle suggested the possibility of a hidden scarf of spotless satin, the secret gift of some ladye fayre. It might have been his pocket-handkerchief though.

Each knight was armed with a lance with the broom part broken off, which he waved in salute to the Queen of Love and Beauty.

"By my halidome!" quoth Sir Cooke de Puddingwell, picking a leg of cold chicken, and stirring up his fiery barb so that a little touch of spring-halt might not be too visible, "an' I take not six rings to-day, call me churl."

"Gramercy for thy liberality, gentle sir," retorted the Viscount Morgeejee, who had just bought some peanuts.

"By the rood! an' ye shall prove the boast to the death, an' our lady wills it," quoth Sir Blessingen, brushing a fly from the place where his courser had been galled by the collar when ploughing. At this moment the New York heralds appeared in the centre of the field, and proceeded to publish the *Personals* of the Coming contest. One of them lifted up his voice, and said, —

"Here ye all! If the four gentlemen who rode up to Chipmunk this morning wish to continue their acquaintance with the four ladies who love them; let them at once address themselves to obtaining rings."

Then all the heralds joined in the chorus of "Largesse, noble knights, largesse;" and then retired to play seven-up behind a nobleman's carriage with "U. S. Ambulance" inscribed upon its panel.

Passing one half of his apple to the nearest lady, and putting the other half into his pocket, Captain Munchausen took a standing position upon his barrel, and says he, —

"Let the Tournamong proceed!"

Away hobbled all the knights at the word, in a series of uneven hops best adapted to the infirmities of the mettled Arabians they bestrode; making directly for the first post of rings and aiming with their lances to cary off one ring at least.

Sir Cooke de Puddingwell almost had one, when his blooded mare took fright at a "chignon" in the range of his vision, and staggered horror-stricken against Sir Render's Hambletonian, with such a shock to that knight, as caused his helmet to fall off and reveal a lunch of two roast apples on his head. Seeing their advantage, the Viscount Morgeejee and Sir Blessingen made a gallant push for the other post, amid the plaudits of the nobility and gentry; but Sir Cooke and Sir Render, recovering, were there, too, as quickly, and the wriggling of all their horses was as one sound.

"By the Mass! Sir Viscount," said Sir Blessingen, hotly, "an' thou keep not thy lance from the small of my back, I will make thee cry Gramercy!"

"Ay, by my halidome!" quoth Sir Cooke de Puddingwell, "an' thou keep not thy steed, Sir Blessingen, from trying to sit in my lap, I will serve thee an' thou wert a varlet!"

Here Captain Munchausen, who had just drawn a pair of clean white socks over his hands to be more genteel, once more arose upon his barrel, and says he, —

"The first round of the Tournamong is over. Five minutes for refreshments, by 'r lady!"

I turned to Villiam, whose inferior Sixth Ward nature had become dumfounded at the courtly display, and said I, —

"Well, my Iron Duke, how standest thou the feverish excitement of the scene?"

"Hum!" says Villiam, musingly, "methinks I see the Arabian Nights of my childhood. Methinks," says Villiam, historically, "that mine eyes behold the Field of the Cloth of Gold, — after it has suspended speshie payment."

I was about to rejoin, when the ringing of a dinner-bell by an extra herald brought the knights in line again, and the tournamong raged with renewed force. Owing to the fact that the steed of Sir Cooke, while lunching upon the tempting tail of Sir Blessingen's steed bit unexpectedly upon the raw, the latter nobleman suddenly went to the front, with a plunge like a huge grasshopper, and, striking full against the first ring post, brought it crashing to the ground.

"A foul blow, by my halidome!" shouted Sir Cooke, impatiently striving to break his charger of the habit of walking on three legs, which it had acquired in the grocery business.

"By the Mass! an' thou sayest so thou liest, base churl!" roared the agitated Sir Blessingen, doubly frantic at having jammed his fingers and found his pockets picked of four gingernuts.

In a moment all was in confusion; and to add to the dreadful splendors of the scene, Sir Render Awdye, in bending eagerly down from his saddle to look for rings, made such a display of a pair of suspenders as caused several ladies to faint on the spot.

In short, the tournamong was over; and, after amicably uniting forces to chastise three members of the freed-negro race who had been heard to laugh, the knights and spectators went their ways, and we returned thoughtfully to the chateau.

Can it be, my boy, that a people who thus retain all the usages and hardihood of knighthood, really lack any radical essential to suit the pleasure of the CHASE?

Yours, inquisitively,
ORPHEUS C. KERR.

LETTER XIX.

PAYING A HANDSOME TRIBUTE TO WOMAN; INTRODUCING A BRIDE, AND PREPARATION FOR THE BRIDAL; GIVING THE ORIGIN AND PLAN OF CHIPMUNK CATHEDRAL; SKETCHING A GRAND SOUTHERN RITUALISTIC WEDDING; AND SHOWING HOW OUR CORRESPONDENT WAS ONCE "UP TO SNUFF."

CHIPMUNK COURT HOUSE, June 18, 1868.

FROM those passionate days when the arms and feats of Woman had so wrought upon the feelings of a British army that it toasted the Maid of Orleans, there has been a marked tendency amongst owners of mothers-in-law to let the Toast be Dear Woman. But we must remember, that, in the time of Joan of Arc, protracted celibacy often subjected the unwedded fair one to the rigors of a convent; and, rather than come to that, many a maiden was willing to accept a suitor who was half-a-loafer, upon the principle that half-a-loaf was better than nun. The English troops may have regarded Miss Joan's late proceedings in the light of a loaf; and, having cut her off from the latter, felt justified in toasting her over the same fire with their stake. At any rate, the historical precedent from which modern mother-in-lawyers take inspiration for their malevolent convivial *mots*, has no force at all for those genuine admirers and respecters of the sex who ask no toasting for the modest, domestic young woman who is home-maid bred.

If, in following my mention of the heroine of Orleans with the name of Matilda Munchausen, I should also greet the latter as a Maid of Four Liens, — because at least four liens are held against the estates of the Munchausens by low Northern persons having mortgages thereon, — there are those who would accuse me of greatly exasperating them with a hideous pun. I think, therefore, that it will be well for me to respect the unhappy prejudices of such critics, and save them from a degrading display of their bad temper, by not doing so. Suffice it to say, then, that the lady of the ancient Southern chateau, which I am now aiding to reconstruct, is certainly worthy the proud old name of Penruthers, attained by her to-day in the bond and mortgage of matrimony; nor shall the apparent slight coolness of herself and her family toward me keep back my delicate tribute of admiration on such an occasion as the present. Her chamber in the luxurious Munchausen chateau has hitherto been immediately above mine; and, early this morning, while she, with all her windows open (to disguise the absence of a whole pane of glass from any one of them), was getting ready for the bridal, I overheard her softly singing to herself the following graceful little

CHANSON.

Avez vous mon parapluie?
Celui-là, ou celui-ci?

Il n'a celui de personne :
N'a-t-il pas son pantalon ?

Qui a soin de mon cheval ?
A quel pied a-t-il mal ?
Je suis venu près de vous,
Il est venu près de nous.

Manger trop est dangereux :
Bonne renommée vaut mieux,
Il fait un bon ordinaire —
Pensez-vous que je puisse faire ? *

* I take these sprightly lines (probably one of the lighter lyrics of Hugo) to be expressive of pleasant girlish badinage. The young bride jocosely asks her lover if he has her umbrella (synonymous with parasol at the South just now). To which it is answered, that he has not; — that he really has but the clothes he stands in. This is the French way of stating that he is very poor. Then the bride, in the same spirit again, wants to know who is to take care of her pet saddle-horse after she is married, and attend to its ailings; as the creature must now come very near to two persons instead of one? But, in the last quatrain, woman's heart at once accepts the situation frankly, contends that a good name is better than gluttonous living, hints that those are rich enough who have the former, and archly asks a compliment for the fair philosopher. The lines may be freely rendered into English, thus, —

> Have you my umbrella there ?
> This or that one — I don't care !
> He has no one's; his is thus,
> Propria quæ maribus.
>
> Who will tend my pony, now ?
> Tell which foot is sorest, too ?
> As I come the nearer thee,
> He to us should nearer be.
>
> Peril 'tis to eat too much, —
> Better honest name than such;
> He fares well who sticks unto it :
> Do you think that I can do it ?

The translation scarcely does justice to the gracefully coquettish spirit of the original, but conveys its sense. — ED.

(Nonsense! The "lines" are merely so many hap-hazard and disconnected phrases from the "Exercises" of some French Grammar, or Reader! — PUBLISHER.)

Unconscious of a hearer, the lovely songstress was taking French-leave, so to speak, of her girlish days. As the student returned from a college where he has acquired great facility in misunderstanding Latin will occasionally sing bits of supposed verse in that language in a way to sadden everybody, so did this affianced Southern bride warble the plaintive lines she had, perhaps, learned at her happy early boarding-school, where French was the language if desired by parents. And while I listened to the melodious strain, and imagined the beautiful strainer dropping a final tear to the memory of her sunny days of girlhood, I could not but envy the haughty bridegroom destined to have her for his own; and wonder how the mischief he was ever going to support her.

Even while I mused thus, the sound of another voice saluted my ears from below the casement,—the voice of Captain Munchausen, who, in consequence of an accident to his ancestral treasury, had just borrowed three dollars from the aged colored seneschal, of the chateau, to aid in the approaching nuptial pageant.

"Seneschal," says he, coldly, "if this is all that the varlet Yankees have given thee in largesse, I will e'en place it in my gipsire for want of more."

The seneschal appeared to heave a sigh, and says he, "Dat's all I got, Mars'r Captain; and I hope Mars'r 'll let me go and vote for de Convention dis mornin' before Miss 'Tilda gits married."

His former owner scowled thoughtfully at the ignorant

black, and says he, "Seneschal, what is this Convention to do?"

The venerable freedman scratched his head, and says he: "I don't know, Mars'r, but I b'lieve it's to get up a new Consumption for de State."

"Ha! ha! ha!" laughed the scornful Southron, with horrible bitterness. "You mean Constitution, poor gorilla; and tell me now, thou sorry knave, what is a Constitution?"

"I don't know 'zactly, Mars'r Captain," says the aged negro, "and dat's a fac'. I 'spect, though, dat its some kind of canonderdrum out o' de Bible."

"And these," hissed the proud Confederacy through his set teeth, "these are the creatures who are to—ha! ha!—rule the down-trodden South, while we, her mortgaged white sons, are dissss-feranchised!! Why, yonder losel military scopion, from the plebeian North, shall show more intelligence."

Here the disfranchised knight hailed one of our Mackerels, who chanced to be on guard near the porch, and says he,—

"Tell us, thou reptile, what is a Constitution?"

"Consteechooshun is it, ye mane!" says the soldier, in a voice that had often reached the North Poll, "Sure, and its a bit av paper that every Amairikin citeezen signs whin he declares his intintions."

At this moment Captain Munchausen was seized with a

violent cough; and says he, "O — ah — yes, I see. But you can retire, sirrah."

"As for you, Satan," says he, making a pass at the aged seneschal with the oiled-silk umbrella-sheath, which he carried as a purse, "if you attempt to vote I'll discharge you."

But the seneschal, in return, made a pass at him with the dust-pan, and peevishly asked for his money again; whereupon the passionate knight called aloud for military aid from the United States; and, but for the prompt mediation of the Mackerel, the long expected War of Races must have commenced at the South.

Hark, though! The pewter spoon has been hung upon its wire in the dish-pan, and the great bell of the chateau, thus reconstructed, rings a merry peal for the bridal. Let all political differences, my boy, be lost in the fragrant smoke of Hymen's torch, while I skip over intervening incidents and take you directly to the wedding.

Inasmuch as the principal sacred edifice of this financial metropolis was torn down, during the recent Federal carnage, by our military Vandals (because some thirteen unconquerable Confederacies in spectacles occupied the turret with duck-guns, and created disturbances in our ranks), the only fashionable church now standing is composed of the body of an old Dry Dock omnibus, presented by wealthy Southern exiles in New York, with a steeple over the door-end formed successively of a cracker-box, a fish-keg, and a nine-shilling gothic clock. This stately triumph of Noah's

Arkitechture is said to look much like the famous English church of St. Mary-Axe, but, as it is not quite so large, it is very properly called St. Mary-Hatchet; and here, in this cathedral, with a spacious blackberrying-ground around it, the marriage of P. Penruthers and M. Munchausen would have been solemnized, but for the high-handed conduct of a prominent church-officer. To speak plainly, it is the custom of the sexton of the cathedral to occupy the driver's seat of the former omnibus during the service, and, by means of the strap wound about his leg, permit none of the congregation to open the door and slip out while the collection is being taken up. When applied to by the brothers of the bride, this embittered official agreed to admit the party to the cathedral; but utterly refused to think of such a thing as letting them out again without a collection for his own benefit. This, of course, settled the matter, as the Rothschilds still mysteriously refrain from subscribing to the new Munchausen Loan; and it was decided that the ceremony should take place, according to the forms of the Ritualists, at the chateau.

Nowhere save at the South, at this particular period of Reconstruction, is a Ritualistic wedding seen in all its pomp. That is to say — nowhere else are so many Pompeys present. As I gazed to-day at the row of sable retainers around the nobility and gentry at the wedding, and wondered whom they expected to collect their next quarter's wages from, it struck me that the Sheriff's writual had its element there. Thus do wordly thoughts intrude upon the most solemn scenes, and I merely mention it as an original discovery.

Captain Villiam Brown and I had been invited, on condition of lending clean collars, and furnishing a box of candles for the ceremony; and when we entered the saloon of the chateau and gazed through our pieces of Smoked Glass upon the scene, the brilliancy of the latter made us wink. The mangle, brought in from the kitchen and converted into a covered table by means of a white counterpane, bore some twenty burning tallow-candles in soda-water bottles. Above it trembled a tasteful canopy, made from the top of a sugar-barrel, draped with evergreens. Behind it, on the wall, hung a picture representing the arrest of one of the early Christians for debt. At the table stood the Ritual rector, in chasuble made of the stuff left over from the two large blue cotton umbrellas which Villiam and I had given to be made into a bridal-gown and hoop skirt for the lady of the chateau. To the right were a band of boy-choristers, from the local Orphan Asylum; on the left, a company of acolytes from the neighboring County House; still farther to the left was the choir, composed of the Mackerel Brass Band with his night-key bugle, and the aged colored seneschal, with a large comb wrapped in paper; around the room sat the family and guests, on inverted peach-baskets; and, facing the table and rector, stood the lordly Pendragon Penruthers, Esquire, and his Southern bride!

You can form no idea of the knightly and chivalric aspect of this people, my boy, save in a courtly pageant like this. You at the North are chiefly familiar with Southern medical students, who, instead of using the ancient lance for artillery, use the modern lancet for ill artery; but, if you want to see what Chivalry really is, at the South, come gaze through my Smoked Glass at this scene of Ritualism.

The Ritual rector now intoned a Nux Vomica, accompanied in a slow adagio movement by night-key bugle and comb; and then, looking steadfastly at the couple, snuffed out two candles with his fingers. This signified that all their past separate lives, save debts and mortgages, were extinguished by marriage. Bride and groom bowed assent; the acolytes filed between them and the table; and the Ritual rector snuffed-out the remaining candles, — which signified that the family couldn't afford to let them burn any longer, as they had no others in the house.

Next, in time to slow music by the choir, the Ritual rector lifted from the interior of the mangle a living wren, its little feet and wings tied, and itself lying upon about ten cents' worth of ice. What this chilled wren signified I could not understand exactly, but bride and groom again bowed very low.

"Then I pronounce you mortgaged to each other for life," says the Ritual rector, commencing to eat an apple (significant of Eve's transgression), and the boy-choristers at once began a solemn dance about the pair, singing

SOLO.

"Thus man takes a mortgage on woman for life,
With interest due in good faith from the wife;
And if she don't pay it, her husband she'll force
To quickly foreclose with a suit for divorce.

CHORUS.

"—— Be happy, be worthy, be thrifty and wise;
Take all the good chances of Time as he flies;
And still be your doctrine, or healthy, or sick,
Rit-u-al, rit-u-al, rit-u-al-is-tic."

This concluded the impressive ceremony. The twain had been made one, for better, for worse, in life and in debt; and, after the usual congratulations, the whole party repaired in procession to the *salle à manger*, where a wedding-banquet of hoe-cake and United States rations awaited us. The ritual rector came with the rest, in high spirits, being apparently affected by some sort of congestion of the brain, which led him into the wild fancy that he was to be paid something for his services; but as the moments rolled on, and the knightly brothers of the bride still dodged him around peach-baskets and behind doors, he gradually settled into hopeless melancholy, and finally went home to his starving family.

Not knowing where they might get their next meal, the bride and her haughty lord ate heartily; giving me opportunity to observe their happiness without peril of resentment for my staring. And, as I studied the spacious cheek of Matilda, memory went back to other days in the sunny South, when I, myself, had been near offering hand and heart to a belle no less worth ringing. But, *alas! alas!* one evening I was

UNDECEIVED.

All hailed her a parlor Calypso,
   The Syren Supreme of the throng,
Who dazzled with jewels and satins,
   And wooed as they floated along.

Her locks were like night in the tropics,
   Her brow shamed the lily in white;
Her eyes were two oceans of darkness
   Reflecting two oceans of light.

Her lips were the coraline portals,
   The shrine of a heaven of bliss,
That e'en might entice the immortals
   To turn, and be lost in a kiss.

Her garment, in folds dropping lustre
   Trailed softly in ripple and curl,
Seem'd wrought from the wave of a water
   Whose azure had melted a pearl.

One hand reap'd a harvest of ringlets,
   The other ruled grace at her side;
Her form was the form of a maiden,
   In crown of full womanly pride.

I knew her — had known her from childhood;
   Yet, such is the magical spell
Of Beauty enthroned o'er her subjects,
   I dared not salute Anabel.

But Thought spurns the bonds of the human,
   And e'en as I gazed at her there,
I dream'd of a day in the future,
   Of all my young days the most fair.

For, had she not wept at our parting?
    And had she not blush'd when we met
I saw my white rose on her bosom,
    And knew that she could not forget.

'Mid dancing, and gay conversation,
    And planning of new loves around,
I stood there alone with my idol,
    Like Silence ghost-brooding in sound.

What though she smiled others to Heaven
    With lips that were zephyr'd with mirth,
When mine was the droop of the lashes
    That gave me my heaven on earth!

At last, when the voice of a singer
    Came sweet through the tapestried door,
Her courtiers took leave of their Empress,
    And swept o'er the velveted floor.

They left her — she would not go with them,
    And I, in the red curtain's glow,
Was thrilled with such loving emotions
    As none but a lover can know.

I thought, in my joy, to surprise her;
    But paused, as I lifted a fold,
And saw her draw forth from her bosom
    A quaint little casket of gold.

The horrors of jealousy smote me —
    The face of a Rival! thought I;
But scarce had a minute flown over,
    When more was exposed to my eye.

The casket was stealthily opened,
    A hand shed its whiteness within,
And forth from its secret recesses
    Brought something of silver, or tin.

She dipp'd it low down in the casket—
　Glanced anxiously round, as in fear,
Then parted her lips in a moment,
　And plunged it between with a smear!

I saw it, recoiling in horror!
　One glimpse of the scene was enough;
The thing in her mouth was a "Dipper,"
　The casket, a casket of *snuff*.

Oh! what was the glow of her blushes,
　Oh! what was the glance of her eye?
The flush of a deep dissipation,
　The fire that but sparkled to die!

My vision of loveliness faded,
　My passion was turn'd to disdain;
I crept from the place like a shadow,
　And never shall enter again.

Ah, well! such memories have no business at a Munchausen wedding, my boy; and to the latter let us return without farther reminiscence.

When evening came, the great bell of the chateau called us out to the lawn, to witness a surprise in the way of fireworks; and when, at a given signal from Captain Munchausen, the torch was applied to a school-house recently erected by vulgar Yankee capital for the freed-negro race, the display was really creditable.

Here let me take leave of the pageant, while yet its glory must be dazzling every eye. The union of two loving hearts is a topic to which one poor goose-quill never yet did justice,— a whole goose being requisite for the purpose. Will these two be any less happy because they must go to the Almshouse pretty soon? Will a shadow rest upon their united lives because a rash Collector of Income Taxes committed suicide here last evening, shortly after conversing with some of the leading men of the place concerning their gains during the past year? Let us hope not. Let us trust that, as they gradually starve to death — their love for each other as profound as their hatred of the scorpion North which still refuses six months' credit, — they may find in each other's company additional courage to scorn negro-suffrage and heap fresh contumely upon the head of any Northern man who would seek to rescue them from the first-mentioned consummation.

Yours, ritually,

ORPHEUS C. KERR.

LETTER XX.

RECORDING A DAY'S EXCURSION UP THE POTOMAC; ANALYZING A STRAWBERRY FESTIVAL, AND REPORTING SOME OF THE ORATIONS AT SUSPER COLLEGE COMMENCEMENT.

CHIPMUNK COURT HOUSE, June 26, 1868.

THE human soul — how sensitive a thing it is! especially before its owner hears from his poor relations, or has a wife subject to sick-headache. How keenly alive it is to every impression of Change, even when the latter is not change for five dollars! How quickly will it swell, or collapse, at the least variation in the chromatic scales of that instrument of piano and forte emotions which we call Home!

You return to the latter after the day's business; and, before you have seen or spoken to a soul there, a subtle sensibility to some unpleasant change in it comes sickeningly over you. In another moment you detect a carpet-bag and bandbox in the hall, and then you know that your wife's mother has come to spend a week with you. Regaining the same Home after a brief trip to the country, there is something in the aspect of the very front-door that inexplicably impresses you with a delightful sense of home's sweetest tranquillity. You enter, and are informed that your eldest unmarriageable sister-in-law has decided to defer her visit until next summer. So it is that some mysterious intuitive intelligence of the human soul — that possession coming by nature to every man save the New Jerseyman — detects the sadder and happier domestic changes for us long before the material senses can act. Thus it is that we need no telling to comprehend, that the man with the pew-bill has been waiting for us in the parlor nearly half an hour.

And how much stronger is the vibration of this fine instinct, when the very loudest component element of a home has gone out of it! There has been a Marriage in the house, and the merest stranger asks no telling to be aware of it before he has been within the door five minutes. There is no more poking of a head in curl-papers over the baluster of the second-story stairs every time the street-bell rings. There is no more screeching of alternate hymn-verses and "Duchess of Gerolstein" hand-organ airs through the third-story hall until eleven o'clock every morning. There is no more slapping of infant brothers to stop their crying for tumbling downstairs, and make them learn not to take their sister's back-hair off the bureau and use it for a ball another time. There is no more driving of nails (of her fingers) on the piano-forte, with all the parlor-windows open, at what a merciful Providence intended to be the quietest hour of the evening. There is no more standing on the front-stoop and taking three-quarters of an hour to scream and giggle a good-night to the departing Young Man already half-way to the corner, when five single gentlemen on the same block, who *must* get up at five o'clock in the morning, are trying to swear themselves to sleep. No; there has been a Marriage in the house, and the yearning souls of the survivors plaintively acknowledge that the cessation of so much sweetness and noise makes it seem just like Sunday, at home.

The late Confederate pageant of a Ritualistic marriage has left the ancient chateau of the Munchausens so lonely for me that I have made a flying excursion to Succotash Court House, where even orations by collegians are better than no noise at all. On the morning after the wedding, when Pendragon Penruthers, Esquire, his bride and brothers-in-law, started for a day's bridal-tour of the Charitable Institutions of Chipmunk Court House, Captain Villiam Brown and I were directed to remain in the kitchen with the aged seneschal and help clean the knives; but Villiam's unhappy disposition to want nobody to get married but himself had made him such poor company for the occasion, that a sense of there having been a Marriage in the house grew intolerable to me, and I suddenly resolved to take a sail up the Potomac for the day. When I told him of my determination, Villiam was cleaning a costly cast-iron carving-knife, which, as there had been no earthly use for it in the family since the late Vandal war, had grown quite rusty — and says he, —

"Go, my fren', and I will continue the great work of Reconstruction alone until your return. "Ah!" says Villiam, trying the highly-tempered blade on his fingernail, "it is now nearly time for our ten o'clock snub, and that bright being is not here to give it to us."

Perceiving that his Democratic Northern nature drooped in the anticipated absence of those daily affronts to which we were accustomed, I tried to comfort him with the certainty that Lady Penruthers would yet insult us oftener than ever before she finally went away with her lord to his home in the Almshouse; and so greatly did the assurance cheer him that, just previous to my departure, he cleaned a broken and very difficult fork in three minutes.

A brisk walk of about an hour — through plantations so covered with mortgages as to be actually dying because neither son nor heir could get to them — brought me to the landing where the Confederate steamboat, "South C. Bubble," built in South Carolina, awaited such passengers as the captain was willing to trust for their passage-money. The floating palace, in question, had formerly been a coal-barge; but now, by aid of a second-hand cooking-stove, a tin clothes-boiler, a steam-pipe from thence to the hickory pistons of a walking-beam which had been ingeniously manufactured from a large wagon-spring, and a couple of U. S. ambulance-wheels at the sides, she made the best steamer that it was possible to run on credit.

My payment of my passage in actual money threw the entire crew into a profuse perspiration, and caused the captain to exhibit temporary signs of apoplexy; yet, at the proper moment, the great naval commander was sufficiently recovered to mount one of the wheel-houses, (half a cheese-box), draw forth his galvanized chronometer, and signal the engineer to turn on the steam from the clothes-boiler. Wush-wush-wush-h-h went the ambulance-wheels, high curled the smoke from the stack of old hats acting as a smoke-pipe, and along moved the majestic vessel, after the manner of a dying swan.

Perceiving, from my payment of fare, and the absence of holes from the elbows and knees of my garments, that I was a scorpion carpet-bagger from the plebeian North, the company on board did not invite me to join in the games of euchre which they were playing for bone-buttons, just abaft the mainstay; and, to keep myself in countenance, I soon repaired to the dissecting-table of the surgeon of the ship, and nearly threw that glassy official into a fit by paying him to make me a strawberry festival.

In coarse Northern cities, a strawberry festival, when gotten-up in aid of some church, or charitable institution, is made as follows: A glass vessel, holding about a pint, is supplied with enough ice to preserve the fruit, and upon the extreme top thereof, two, and sometimes three strawberries are carefully placed. Then, a rich sauce, composed of sherry, a little brandy, a sprig of mint, a slice of orange, a bit of pineapple, and a tall, hollow straw (hence STRAW-berry festival), is poured over the preserved berries, and the festival is ready for church-members. But, at the South, just now, owing to a momentary difference with the Rothschilds, ice is too expensive to be had; so the surgeon of the ship used some fragments of broken glass bottles instead; and, as his nearest approach to sherry and brandy was some molasses and water, the strawberry festival he made for me was not as stimulating as I have known such festivals to be.

In fact, shortly after partaking of this strawberry festival, I was seized with a serious sea-sickness; and as the vessel was stopping just then at Succotash Court House to land those who had come thither to attend the commencement of the celebrated Susper College, I too went ashore to shake off my illness by a passing glimpse of the Confederate educational pageant.

Susper College boasts a faculty composed almost exclusively of Major-General Southern Confederacies who have not yet been hung for pointing and discharging disloyal artillery against the United States of America, and occupies a large wooden building situated upon one of the largest mortgages in the State.. Prior to certain late Federal outrages upon a wealthy and chivalrous people, the Southern youth, attending this institution of learning, wore dress-coats at all hours of the day, and spent nearly as much money for "poker," and other necessaries of life, as would have sufficed to pay the interest on their fathers' debts. During the present season, however, they are attired in coats and continuations, which bear more rags to the acre than ever came before from sowing tares; and when a young student of sixteen, named Lieutenant-Colonel Montmorency, stood upon the ironing-table, used as a rostrum, to deliver his oration, I noticed that his coat was fastened in front with a wooden skewer.

The orations were impassioned, and scholarly appeals in behalf of State rights and Southern sentiment, showing that what the South now needs are independence and capital. Colonel Chilmondely, a fervid young student of thirteen, spoke of Virginia as the Mother of Mortgages, and drew a fine ideal picture of the future days when all her debts should be paid off, and her railroads and her colleges able to borrow some more money. Major Ilfracombe, aged twelve, and wearing a brass-headed nail for a scarf-pin spoke eloquently of the State-debt, which, he said, like the mighty Mississippi emptying into the sea, emptied into the Bankrupt Act.

Captain Penremington, aged nine years, urged his brethren to go boldly forth from College into the North, and demand — ay, DEMAND! six months' credit. The time had now arrived when the South should assert herself, and, — in helm and with spear, if necessary, — claim her share of the ill-gotten wealth of the North. (Great sensation.) Let the South say to the North, — "We do not want you yourselves with us; but we have need of your small change, to develop our great resources (tremendous enthusiasm), to educate and exterminate our servile population, and to prepare ourselves for another and mightier struggle with your vandal military scorpions." (Prolonged cheers.) Then, after obtaining the small change, who could doubt that the renovated and newly armed South would

> "As victor exult, or in debt be laid low,
> With her note for six months in the hands of the foe;
> And, leaving in bottle no drop as it came,
> Demand a new deal and begin a new game."

When the enthusiastic applause had subsided, General Hardupton, of South Carolina, mounted the ironing-table, and proceeded to address the Literary Societies of the College upon the "Duties of Citizenship." He told the students that, as citizens of the Republic, it would be their first duty to be devoted exclusively to their own State, which, upon the whole, was the only State in the Union worth mentioning. Let them remember her host of noble sons, who comprised all the United States' Presidents worth speaking about. At present, she was pecuniarily embarrassed, but would yet pass (should the Bankrupt Act be proved Constitutional) from debt into life. In conclusion, he solemnly warned the young man against ever "playing policy" to the detriment of their principal. If the temptation beset them, let them go into the nearest cemetery and consider the examples of those who had preferred to be taken by the knave of spades and await the last trump.*

At the conclusion of these interesting exercises the en-

---

* See address of rebel General Wade Hampton, at the recent "Commencement" of General Lee's Washington College, Va.

thusiasm was unbounded, — some of the worst straw hats I ever saw (made chiefly from the covers of market-baskets) being waved in the air, while the ladies as energetically fluttered the ends of pillow-cases which they carried as handkerchiefs.

Depend upon it, my boy, this proud people only need be trusted in order to become nearly as great a comfort to us as they ever were before. Between sections, as between individuals, there can be no real love without trust; and when next your Southern brethren come walking scornfully into your vulgar Northern stores and boarding-houses, TRUST them, for six months at least; and you will surely get your pay, — if not in this, why, then, in another and a better world to which we are all hastening.

Yours, mediatingly,

ORPHEUS C. KERR.

LETTER XXI.

WHICH DILATES UPON THE MILITARY MIND AS AFFECTED BY SOUTHERN EXPERIENCE; SHOWS HOW A DESERVING SOUTHERN UNIONIST WAS FEARFULLY. AND WONDERFULLY TRIED BY MACKEREL COURT-MARTIAL; AND EXPLAINS HOW CAPTAIN MUNCHAUSEN, BEING RECONSTRUCTED, SENT GREETINGS TO THE UNITED STATES OF AMERICA AND TERMINATED THIS EVENTFUL HISTORY.

CHIPMUNK COURT HOUSE, June 20, 1868.

To the military mind, withdrawn from contemplation of the ensanguined field through a spy-glass, and informed upon application that there are no immediate vacancies in the Custom House, — there is nothing more profoundly interesting than the spectacle of a superior people gradually rising from their first unmitigated astonishment at defeat, and rapidly regaining their original largeness of impressive shirt-collar. The military mind, I say, in its few instances of not being called immediately after a war to illuminate the office of Governor or Secretary of State, finds a weird fascination in this development of a high-toned characteristic of superior blood, and has been known upon certain garrison occasions to grovel ecstatically before so much renewed immensity of aspect. The mechanical effects of martial discipline, and some remembrance of having tended a restaurant in earlier life, frequently conduce to make the American Military mind exquisitely sensitive to that peremptory demand for an attached waiter which continually effulges from a dress-coat mien sufficiently overbearing; and many a brass-buttoned brigadier of our invincible army has paused, as commandant, in some refined Southern town of his conquest, only to fall a prostrate valet before the large-sized demeanor of its most insulting and respectable citizens.

These reflections coursed pleasantly through *my* mind, and caused me to wink knowingly with my mind's eye, as I stood in the little encampment, on the lawn of the chateau, and listened to the talk of our reconstructing National troops. There was one Mackerel cheerfully trying the range of his gun, by firing a few experimental bullets at a member of the freed-negro race on an adjacent fence; and, just as the redeemed freedman put down his hoe-cake on a post to see what was in his hat, he turned immediately to another Mackerel, and says he, —

"It's naygurs, the like of him convanient to the fince, that they kape us here to purtect, whin the war's over intirely. An, sure, why couldn't they lave the black craytures to the gintleman that ouns them, and lave us to go home an' vote?"

The other Mackerel stopped dealing out rations to the aged seneschal, who had just come with a basket for the Munchausen family-breakfast, and says he, —

"Why, Antonio, nobody ouns them now. They're free, and will be a comin' and takin' the bread out of our mouths next."

Antonio only paused a moment, to kick the seneschal, and says he, —

"It's bate them I would, if I was the gintleman, and then see if it's us white min that would interfere. Ah, but it's the rale gintleman he is, up at the house yonder; an' I've not seen the like of him since I came over. He doesn't be spakin' to common folks the like of us, at all, sure; and that was the way with Lord Dunlaff when I tinded his horses at home."

I turned from the spot, musingly, my boy, and it occurred to me that there is possibly a greater capacity for popular influence in cheek than in mouth.

But why lingers my pen around these beautiful incidents, like a bee around flowers, when the stern duty of the historian requires it to skip all the fragrant poetry of human nature, and make note only of its scents-less pros and cons? Why dallies my forgetful quill with what may be termed foreign phlox, when it should be busy with something closely approximate to its native goose?

Let Themis — Titanic Goddess, as Hesiod would have her — shrink to the dimensions of a little girl with a "chignon," and hide her increased head, while I relate to an excited universe the details of Captain Villiam Brown's court-martial-inquest, in the case of a Southern Union man of Chipmunk, accused of having remarked, that he cared not what others might say, but, as for him, give him liberty or give him death.

It did not appear that this observation had any particular

application to anything excessively national; in fact, the said observation was believed by some to have been merely a quotation from Patrick Henry, and having reference solely to a question of African choice between emancipation and freedom; but Villiam at once convened a Mackerel court-martial in the back kitchen, with an intelligent Mackerel for Judge Advocate; and when the prisoner was brought in with his counsel, Villiam frowned majestically upon him from the mangle, and says he, —

"Prisoner at the refrigerator, you are arraigned on a charge of having uttered incendiary words, and are here to take your trial for better or worse. Have you any reason to show why sentence of death should not be pronounced upon you?"

Here the counsel for the defence arose hastily from a wash-tub, and says he, —

"Now this is really —"

"Silence, sarah!" says Villiam, sternly, "and don't try to bully this court, which knows more about law," says Villiam, emphatically, "than ever you read of in Story. You musn't try any of your bullying here, sarah!"

The counsel for the defence merely wished to state —

The Judge Advocate suggested that it was scarcely worth while to heed this wretched man's miserable drivel; but if the convicted traitor at the refrigerator would not at once confess himself guilty of arson against the government, the witnesses must appear.

Therefore, J. Smith, being duly sworn, testified that he

had known the prisoner at the refrigerator for some time, and always believed him to be a fiend in human form; had frequently supposed him to be a brute in human shape, and remembered he had once asked a man at a deaf and dumb asylum if he did not think so too. Could not tell precisely the hour on each day when he had spoken of the accused as a demon in human habiliments, but thought it was every hour; the prisoner had owed him four dollars and a half for three years.

Counsel for defence put on his spectacles, and says he,—
"But how did—"

Here the Judge Advocate wished to inform the caricature of humanity then speaking, that he must not try any of his low bullying here, because it wouldn't do. He must not attempt to intimidate this court with his vaporings.

The following witness, Alonzo Tubbs, being sworn, deposed that he had known the prisoner at the refrigerator four years, and must admit that he regarded him as a monster in human guise; had at times pronounced him to be a modern Nero, and often thought he resembled a wolf in sheep's clothing; had spoken to prisoner once as to the feasibility of his lending seven shillings for a few days, and had been refused in traitorous language.

The counsel for the defence drew a paper from one of his pockets, and says he,—
"Will the witness inform the court—"

The Judge Advocate desired to know whether the ravings of the maddened blusterer then howling were to be longer permitted? He must be taught that this was no place to bring his threatening airs. His braggadocia would not do here.

Abel Drinker, being properly sworn, stated that he had known deceased often, and believed the counsel for the defence to be capable of any crime when under the influence of liquor —

Here the counsel for the defence tore his hair, and says he, —

"I protest against —"

"Silence, sarah!" says Villiam, "or I'll try you for the assassination of your father. You can't bully this court, sarah!"

The Judge Advocate could not pause to mention that the calumnious pettifogger had several times attempted the life of his mother, but would consent to the introduction of his first witness — not in obedience to any of his bullying, though.

Doctor Gigby, being sworn, affirmed that he had attended the prisoner at the refrigerator during a recent illness, during which the said prisoner had complained of seeing monkeys; at one stage of the disease heard him say "Our noble President" very distinctly —

"Ah!" says Villiam, with such a start that he nearly fell into the mangle, "what was that?"

"He said, 'Our noble President' very distinctly."

"Hum!" says Villiam. "If he said, that, sarah, I

hereby squash the indictment, and declare him man and wife. Let the counsel for the defence be committed for a further hearing."

And, the court being therefore instantly dissolved, we repaired to the *salle à manger*, where Captain Munchausen, Matilda, P. Penruthers, the Provisional Governor, and an aged Confederacy (who introduced the stately fashion of wearing an overcoat and muffler indoors, by reason of being temporarily deficient in the frock-coat and shirt-collar department), awaited us at the groaning supper-board.

"Gen-til-men," said the Provisional Governor, disguising a sneer in a highly unnatural cough, "let me introduce General Lately (as slightly distinguished from General Early), whom we propose to install as President of Cotton Seminary to-morrow."

"Hum!" says Villiam, attentively eying the aged stranger through his bit of Smoked Glass. "Methinks I have seen that being behind a musket, propelling glossy missiles toward the United States of America."

"You have, my man," responded the venerable Washington, in a deep bass tone; "but I am now a cultivator of earth's teeming bosom, and have forgiven everything. I have advised those who have surrendered their muskets, to fire no more at present; but rather to give up slavery for the time being, and pay the freedmen six dollars yearly for their labor."

"And I," said the Provisional Governor, returning from a brief absence, "have just directed the troops on the lawn to march away at once, by authority of our noble President; for my brother is now sufficiently reconstructed to dispense with the military — who," said the Governor, casually, "have been ordered to leave their rations behind with our seneschal."

"Furthermore," exclaimed Captain Munchausen, rising with dignity from a plate of biscuit marked "U. S." — "furthermore, my sister can no longer endure the presence of Vandals drenched in the gore of her forefathers, and your immediate flight from the chateau will be a cause of family congratulation."

Here Matilda turned toward us, so that we could see the new buttons on her dress; and a dreary voice, which seemed to say something about "them nasty Yankees," was heard to float tenderly upon the twilight air.

Villiam and I moved simultaneously toward the door, and says Villiam, —

"Tell me, sarah, what message shall we convey to the United States of America?"

"Tell them," said Captain Munchausen advancing, supported by the Provisional Governor and the aged Confederacy, who had just hauled a couple of muskets from under the table, "tell them that Munchausen is fully reconstructed, and will shortly demand a bottle of Pardon for the patriot Jefferson Davis."

"But, my Chevalier Bayard," said I, in bewilderment, "this Reconstruction is only a Congressional experiment."

"Tell them," said Captain Munchausen, suddenly struck with extreme deafness, "that the sunny South offers peace to the whole country, and will shortly be prepared (in consideration of a few rations and six months' credit for female wearing apparel), to recognize the North as equals."

It rained drearily as Captain Villiam Brown and I set out to overtake the conic section of the Mackerel Brigade, already on its march for the railway station; and as the great drops drove each other through my clothing, I earnestly wished for at least as much pardon in a tumbler as would refract a spoon. I mentioned as much to Villiam, and says he, —

"Pardons, my fren', as there is no bar to them in this sunny clime, and as they seem to be dispensed in accordance with the lick .'er law — Ah!" says Villiam, pausing suddenly, "what's this?"

It was a miserably dilapidated roadside house, through the windows of which a feeble light and the voices of men singing came out upon the thickening darkness of the night. Moving softly to the half-open door, we looked in, and beheld many members of the freed-negro race kneeling, in the wretched room, around the figure of a one-armed sable soldier of the Union, who, holding a lighted tallow candle in his only hand, beat time with it to the supplication all were singing. Here and there in the kneeling congregation appeared the blue uniform which, in every other attitude than that, had stood out a score of times in the red flash of battle; and, as the voices of homely praise and prayer went up to Him who no less gave blackness to the raven than whiteness to the goose, I thought it was fitting that the light, in its intoning rise and fall, should alternately call from the shadows of a far corner and restore to them again the bust of ABRAHAM LINCOLN.

Yours, reverently,

ORPHEUS C. KERR.

APPENDIX.

APPENDIX.

I.

OPENING ARGUMENT OF MANAGER, THE HON. B. F. BUTLER, IN THE HIGH COURT OF IMPEACHMENT, MONDAY, MARCH 30, 1868.

MR. PRESIDENT AND GENTLEMEN OF THE SENATE: — The onerous duty has fallen to my fortune to present to you, imperfectly as I must, the several propositions of fact and the law upon which the House of Representatives will endeavor to sustain the cause of the people against the President of the United States, now pending at your bar.

The high station of the accused, the novelty of the proceeding, the gravity of the business, the importance of the questions to be presented to your adjudication, the possible momentous result of the issues, each and all must plead for me to claim your attention for as long a time as your patience may endure.

Now, for the first time in the history of the world, has a nation brought before its highest tribunal its chief executive magistrate for trial and possible deposition from office, upon charges of maladministration of the powers and duties of that office. In other times, and in other lands, it has been found that despotisms could only be tempered by assassination, and nations living under constitutional governments even, have found no mode by which to rid themselves of a tyrannical, imbecile, or faithless ruler, save by overturning the very foundation and framework of the government itself. And, but recently, in one of the most civilized and powerful governments of the world, from which our own institutions have been largely modelled, we have seen a nation submit for years to the rule of an insane king, because its constitution contained no method for his removal.

Our fathers, more wisely, founding our government, have provided for such and all similar exigencies a conservative, effectual, and practical remedy by the constitutional provision that the "President, Vice-President, and all civil officers of the United States *shall* be removed from office on impeachment for and conviction of treason, bribery, or other high crimes and misdemeanors." The Constitution left nothing to implication, either as to the persons upon whom, or the body by whom, or the tribunal before which, or the offences for which, or the manner in which this high power should be exercised; each and all are provided for by express words of imperative command.

. . . .

But a single incident only of the business was left to construction, and that concerns the offences or incapacities which are the groundwork of impeachment. This was wisely done, because human foresight is inadequate, and human intelligence fails in the task of anticipating and providing for, by positive enactment, all the infinite gradations of human wrong and sin, by which the liberties of a

APPENDIX. 263

people and the safety of a nation may be endangered from the imbecility, corruption, and unhallowed ambition of its rulers.

It may not be uninstructive to observe that the framers of the Constitution, while engaged in their glorious and, I trust, ever-enduring work, had their attention aroused and their minds quickened most signally upon this very topic. In the previous year only Mr. Burke, from his place in the House of Commons in England, had preferred charges for impeachment against Warren Hastings, and three days before our convention sat he was impeached at the bar of the House of Lords for misbehavior in office as the ruler of a people whose numbers were counted by millions. The mails were then bringing across the Atlantic week by week the eloquent accusations of Burke, the gorgeous and burning denunciations of Sheridan, in behalf of the oppressed people of India, against one who had wielded over them more than regal power. May it not have been that the trial then in progress was the determining cause why the framers of the Constitution left the description of offences because of which the conduct of an officer might be inquired of to be defined by the laws and usages of Parliament, as found in the precedents of the mother country, with which our fathers were as familiar as we are with our own?

In the light, therefore, of these precedents, the question arises, *What are impeachable offences* under the provisions of our Constitution? . . . . . .

I pray leave to lay before you, at the close of my argument, a brief of all the precedents and authorities upon this subject, in both countries, for which I am indebted to the exhaustive and learned labors of my friend, the honorable William Lawrence, of Ohio, member of the Judiciary Committee of the House of Representatives, in which I fully concur and which I adopt.

We define, therefore, an impeachable high crime or misdemeanor to be *one in its nature or consequences subversive of some fundamental or essential principle of government, or highly prejudicial to the public interest, and this may consist of a violation of the Constitution, of law, of an official oath, or of duty, by an act committed or omitted, or, without violating a positive law, by the abuse of discretionary powers from improper motives, or from any improper purpose.*

The first criticism which will strike the mind on a cursory examination of this definition is, that some of the enumerated acts are not within the common-law definition of crimes.   .   .   .   .

Mr. Christian, in his notes to the Commentaries of Blackstone, explains the collocation and use of the words "high crimes and misdemeanors" by saying, —

"When the words 'high crimes and misdemeanors' are used in prosecutions by impeachment, the words 'high crimes' have no definite signification, but are used merely to give greater solemnity to the charge."   .   ..   .

One of the important questions which meets us at the

outset is : Is this proceeding a trial, as that term is understood so far as relates to the rights and duties of a court and jury upon an indictment for crime? Is it not rather more in the nature of an inquest of office?

The Constitution seems to have determined it to be the latter, because, under its provisions the right to retain and hold office is the only subject that can be finally adjudicated; all preliminary inquiry being carried on solely to determine the question and that alone. . . .

A constitutional tribunal solely, you are bound by no law, either statute or common, which may limit your constitutional prerogative. You consult no precedents save those of the law and custom of parliamentary bodies. You are a law unto yourselves, bound only by the natural principles of equity and justice, and that *salus populi suprema est lex*. . . . .

The first eight articles set out in several distinct forms the acts of the respondent in removing Mr. Stanton from office and appointing Mr. Thomas *ad interim*, differing in legal effect in the purposes for which and the intent with which either or both of the acts were done, and the legal duties and rights infringed, and the acts of Congress violated in so doing. All the articles allege these acts to be in contravention of his oath of office, and in disregard of the duties thereof. If they are so, however, the President might have the *power* to do them under the law; still, being so done, they are acts of official misconduct, and, as we have seen, impeachable. . . . . .

This, then, is the plain and inevitable issue before the Senate and the American people : Has the President, under the Constitution, the more than kingly prerogative at will to remove from office, and suspend from office indefinitely, all executive officers of the United States, either civil, military, or naval, at any and all times, and fill the vacancies with creatures of his own appointment, for his own purposes, without any restraint whatever, or possibility of restraint by the Senate or by Congress through laws duly enacted?. The House of Representatives, in behalf of the people, join this issue by affirming that the exercise of such powers is a high misdemeanor in office. If the affirmation is maintained by the respondent, then, so far as the first eight articles are concerned, — unless such corrupt purposes are shown as will of themselves make the exercise of a legal power a crime, — the respondent must go, and ought to go, quit and free. Therefore, by these articles and the answers thereto, the momentous question, here and now, is raised whether the *Presidential office itself* (*if it has the prerogatives and power claimed for it*) *ought, in fact, to exist as a part of the constitutional government of a free people*, while by the last three articles the simpler and less important inquiry is to be determined, whether Andrew Johnson has so conducted himself that he ought longer to hold any constitutional office whatever. The latter sinks to merited insignificance compared with the grandeur of the former. If that is sustained, then a right and power hitherto unclaimed and unknown to the people of the country is engrafted on the Constitution, most alarming in its extent, most corrupting in its influence, most dangerous in its tendencies, and most tyrannical in its exercise. Whoever, therefore, votes "not guilty" on these articles, votes to enchain our free institutions, and to prostrate them at the feet of any man who, being President, may choose to control them.

. . . .

Article ninth charges that Major-General Emory being in command of the military department of Washington, the President called him before him and instructed him that the act of March 2, 1867, which provides that all orders from the President shall be issued through the General of the army, was unconstitutional and inconsistent with his commission, with intent to induce Emory to take orders directly from himself, and thus hinder the execution of the Civil Tenure act, and to prevent Mr. Stanton from holding his office of Secretary of War. If the transaction set forth in this article stood alone, we might well admit that doubts might arise as to the sufficiency of the proof. But the surroundings are so pointed and significant as to leave no doubt on the mind of an impartial man as to the intents and purposes of the President. . . . . Is it not a misdemeanor for the President to assume to instruct officers of the army that the laws of Congress are not to be obeyed? . . . .

Article ten alleges that, intending to set aside the rightful authority and powers of Congress, and to bring into disgrace and contempt the Congress of the United States, and to destroy confidence in and excite odium against Congress and its laws, he, Andrew Johnson, President of the United States, made divers speeches set out therein, whereby he brought the office of President into contempt, ridicule, and disgrace. . . . . .

It may be taken as an axiom in the affairs of nations that no usurper has ever seized upon the legislature of his country until he has familiarized the people with the possibility of so doing by vituperating and decrying it. Denunciatory attacks upon the legislature have always preceded; slanderous abuse of the individuals composing it has always accompanied a seizure by a despot of the legislative power of a country. . . . .

The House of Representatives has done its duty. We has presented the facts in the constitutional manner; we have brought the criminal to your bar, and demand judgment at your hands for his so great crimes. . .

I speak, therefore, not the language of exaggeration, but the words of truth and soberness, that the future political welfare and liberties of all men hang trembling on the decision of the hour.

II.

TESTIMONY IN THE IMPEACHMENT CASE.

GEORGE W. KARSENER, of Delaware, testified that he was an old acquaintance of General Thomas, and that he saw him, about the 7th of March, at a ball, and told him that "the eyes of all Delaware" were upon him, and that he would be expected to stand firm. General Thomas replied that in a day or two he would "kick that fellow out;" by which the witness thought he referred to Mr. Stanton.

William N. Hudson, editor of the "Cleveland Leader," testified to the general accuracy of the report made by him, in connection with another reporter, of the speech made by President Johnson in Cleveland on the 3d of September, 1866. The report made by this witness was made in longhand, and he was subjected to a strict cross-examination as to his ability to report correctly by that method. The witness said that the President was frequently interrupted by the cheers, hisses, and cries of the crowd during the delivery of his speech.

III.

The Washington correspondent of the "New York Herald," under date of April 8, 1868, gave the following copy of a card issued by the Ku-Klux Klan, an ex-rebel secret organization of impecunious political ruffians, —

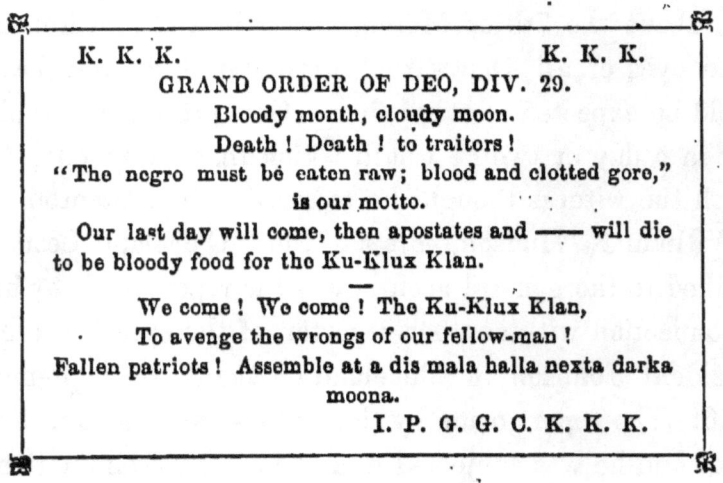

K. K. K.   K. K. K.
GRAND ORDER OF DEO, DIV. 29.
Bloody month, cloudy moon.
Death! Death! to traitors!
"The negro must be eaten raw; blood and clotted gore,"
is our motto.
Our last day will come, then apostates and —— will die to be bloody food for the Ku-Klux Klan.

We come! We come! The Ku-Klux Klan,
To avenge the wrongs of our fellow-man!
Fallen patriots! Assemble at a dis mala halla nexta darka moona.
I. P. G. G. C. K. K. K.

IV.

SPEECH OF JUDGE NELSON, OF TENNESSEE, FOR THE DEFENCE, IN THE HIGH COURT OF IMPEACHMENT, THURSDAY, APRIL 23, 1868.

Mr. Chief Justice and Senators:—I have been engaged in the practice of my profession as a lawyer for the last twenty years, and I have, in the course of my somewhat diversified professional life, argued cases involving life, liberty, property, and character. I have prosecuted and defended every species of crime known to law, from murder in the first degree down to simple assault; but in rising to address you to-day I feel that all the cases in which I was ever concerned sink into comparative insignificance when compared to this one; and a painful sense of the magnitude of the case in which I am now engaged, and of my inability to meet and to defend it as it should be defended, oppresses me as I rise to address you. But I would humbly invoke the Great Disposer of events to give me a mind to conceive, a heart to feel, and a tongue to express those words which should be proper and fitting on this great occasion.

. . . .

If it is true, as is alleged, that the President is guilty of all these things,— if he be guilty of one tithe of the offences which have been imputed to him in the opening argument, and which have been iterated and reiterated in the argument of yesterday and to-day,— then I am willing to confess that he is

> "A monster of such frightful mien,
> That to be hated needs but to be seen."

I am willing to admit that if he was guilty of any of the charges which have been made against him, he is not only worthy the censure of this Senate, but you should place

> "A whip in every honest hand
> To lash him naked through the land."

He should be pointed at everywhere as a monster to be

banished from society, and his name should become a word to frighten children with throughout the land from one end to the other, and when any one should meet him or see him,

> "Each particular hair to stand on end,
> Like quills upon a fretful porcupine."

If he was there, I agree that neither I nor those associated with me can defend him. But who is Andrew Johnson? Who is this man that you have on trial now, and in regard to whom the gaze, not only of "little Delaware," but of the whole Union, and of the civilized world, is directed at the present moment? Who is Andrew Johnson? That is a question which but a few short years ago many of those I now address could have answered with pleasure. Who is Andrew Johnson? Go to the town of Greenville, but a few short years ago a little village in the mountains of East Tennessee, and you will see a poor boy entering that village a stranger, without acquaintance or friends, following an humble mechanical pursuit, scarcely able to read, unable to write, but yet industrious in his profession, honest and faithful in his dealings and having a mind such as the God in heaven implanted in him, and which was designed to be called into exercise and play before the American people.

. . . .

It is true that clouds and darkness gathered around him for the moment, but they soon passed away and were forgotten, —

APPENDIX.

> "Like some tall cliff that lifts its awful form,
> Swells to the vale, and midway meets the storm,
> Though round its breast the rolling clouds are spread,
> Eternal sunshine settles on its head."

Etc., etc., etc.

V.

DEBATE IN THE HOUSE OF REPRESENTATIVES, SATURDAY, MAY 2D, 1868, AS REPORTED IN THE PAPERS OF THE DAY.

THE letter of Mr. Washburne having been read by the clerk, Mr. Donnelly remarked that he was certainly justified in the declarations he had made that the annals of Congress presented no parallel to that letter, and he thought he should establish that there were in that letter twenty-three distinct statements which were twenty-three distinct falsehoods. He should attempt to deal with them as rapidly as possible. Mr. Donnelly went on to explain that he had only received the draft of the bill on the 2d of March; that he had asked leave to introduce it on the 20th; that Mr. Washburne had objected; that he (Mr. Donnelly) had then gone to Connecticut to aid the Republican party in the canvass in that State. He expressed his belief that the objection made by Mr. Washburne had sprung from personal and malicious motives, and remarked that that gentleman could not speak the truth when the truth would best serve his purpose. Having referred to and examined other points in Mr. Washburne's letter, Mr. Donnelly went on to speak of Mr. Washburn, of Wisconsin, as "mousing around" in reference to some other bill.

The SPEAKER interrupted, and said that that was not parliamentary language toward a member who was absent, and who was not involved in the controversy.

Mr. DONNELLY said he would withdraw the remark.

Mr. WASHBURNE (rep.), of Ill., expressed the hope that the party would be allowed to go on.

Mr. DONNELLY, after passing from that point, referred to the charge in Mr. Washburne's letter that his (Mr. Donnelly's) opposition to the bill offered some time since by Mr. Washburn, of Wisconsin, to reduce fares on the Pacific Railroad might be attributed to the fact that he had a free pass to ride over the road, and declared that he had never ridden over a mile of the road, and did not expect to until it was completed from the Mississippi to the Pacific. It would be a consolation then to know that this mighty work had been resisted and opposed by every blatant, loud-voiced, big-breasted, small-headed, bitter-hearted demagogue in all the land. (Laughter on both sides of the chamber.) Referring to the charge made against him in Mr. Washburne's letter of his being an "official beggar," Mr. Donnelly said, "An official beggar!" and that from a gentleman bearing the name which he does! *Et tu Brute!* "An official beggar!" Why, Mr. Speaker, when I entered the State of Minnesota it was Democratic; when I entered the country in which I live it was two to one Democratic.

I asked no office, — I expected none. But the charge comes from such a quarter that I cannot fail to notice it. The gentleman's family are chronic office-beggars. They are nothing if they are not in office. Out of office they are miserable, wretched, God-forsaken, — as uncomfortable as that famous stump-tailed bull in fly-time. (Laughter.) This whole trouble arises from the persistent determination of one of the gentleman's family to sit in this body. Every young male of the gentleman's family is born into the world with "M. C." franked on his broadest part. (Laughter.) The great calamity seems to be that God in his infinite wisdom did not make any of them broad enough to make room for "U. S. S." (Laughter.) There was room for "U. S.," but the other S. slipped over and "U. S. & Co." is the firm. (Laughter.)

The SPEAKER interrupted Mr. Donnelly and reminded him that his language was beyond the usual limit of parliamentary propriety.

Mr. WASHBURNE again expressed his desire that the "party" should be permitted to go on.

Mr. DONNELLY said he was sorry to transgress the proper limits of debate, but the House would perceive that the character of the letter on which he was commenting made him speak under such feeling. . . . . . .

He has lowered by his wholesale, reckless assaults on the honor and character of the members the standard of this body; he has furnished arguments for the wit of Dan Rice;

he has furnished substance for the slanders of the pothouse. Mr. Speaker, I need enter into no defence of the Fortieth Congress. In point of intellect, of devotion to the public welfare, of integrity, of personal character, it will compare favorably with any Congress that ever sat since the foundation of the government. It is illustrated by names that would do honor to any nation in any age of the world. If there be in our midst one low, sordid, vulgar soul, — one barren of mediocre intelligence, — one heart callous to every kindly sentiment and to every generous emotion, — one tongue leprous with slander, — one mouth which is like unto a den of foul beasts, giving forth deadly odors, — if there be here one character which, while blotched and spotted, yet raves and rants, and blackguards like a prostitute, — if there be here one bold, bad, empty, bellowing demagogue, it is the gentleman from Illinois. . . . . . .

Mr. WASHBURNE said: During my entire time of service in this House I have never asked leave to make a personal explanation, and I never expect to. The party from Minnesota has had the letter which I wrote to a gentleman in that State read to the House, and it goes upon the records of the House and on the records of the country, and there it will remain for all time. Every assertion made in that letter is true, and whoever says it is not true states what is false. If I were called upon — and I desire only to say that if I, under any operation of circumstances, were ever called upon, — to make a personal explanation in reply to a member, it would not be to a member who had committed a crime; it would not be to a member who had run away; it would not be to a member who had changed his name; it would not be to a member whose whole record in this House is covered with venality, corruption, and crime.

The SPEAKER reminded the gentleman that his remarks were not parliamentary, etc., etc.

Finally, a committee was appointed to investigate the charges made in Mr. Washburne's letter, and Mr. Donnelly informed the members, that, if it were not unparliamentary, he would ask them all to take a drink!

THE END.

AVERY GLIBUN.

A ROMANCE.

BY ORPHEUS C. KERR.

One volume. 8vo. Cloth, $1.75; or in paper covers, $1.50.

From the Round Table.

"—— with all the highly-wrought interest of sensational fiction, yet with a delicacy that remains unsullied by associations an inferior writer would have avoided as the only means of preserving the purity of his pages, the story leads us through a diversity of scenes which the keen observation and educated eye of the artist alone could put before us — the foibles of the *nouveaux riches*, of the shopkeeping and political aristocracy of New York; the penetralia of Bohemia, of the Albany lobby and the Five Points; of the theatres and newspaper offices and gambling-hells of the city; the parlors of refinement and wealth, and of rich vulgarity; vice in purple and fine linen about the green cloth, and vice in squalor and nakedness in the groggeries of Cow Bay; knavery of high and low degree — a phantasmagoric view of metropolitan life, with such resources of the incongruous, grotesque, and pitiful, of hilarity and tenderness, as even Mr. Dickens has not more strikingly merged. And it is difficult to determine wherein the author's power is greatest. His constructive skill, his dramatic effect, his satirical insight, his fervid descriptions of scenes of grandeur and of horror, his humor, wit, pathos, the depths of passion, of sympathy, even of tenderness, — the combination of these attests a more universal genius, a larger nature, than we supposed was to be found among American novelists."

. . . It is the work of a ripe intellect, and to it the author has given his maturest powers, and his long, unwearied labor. We welcome it to a high place in our permanent literature, and recognize it as one of the very ablest novels that the last decade has produced. — *N. Y. Citizen.*

. . . We have determined to read it, for the reason that no "puff" of the book has yet appeared in print, notwithstanding the fact that the author's position as a journalist affords him unusual opportunites for securing favorable mention of his book by the press. — *N. Y. Com. Advertiser.*

. . . In some parts it is worthy of Dickens, or Wilkie Collins, or of Anthony Trollope. — *Memphis Avalanche.*

. . . As a satirist, the author reminds us of Addison. His satire is keen without malevolence, and witty without spleen. As an interpreter of the language of action, tone, and gesture, he is equalled only by Dickens. — *Rochester Union.*

. . . To Mr. Newel (Orpheus C. Kerr) we unhesitatingly accord a place second to no other American novelist, and there are few upon the other side of the water who in one work of fiction have displayed a more marvellous and versatile genius. — *Lafayette (Ind.) Courier.*

. . . The scene in the chamber of the dying Bohemian, Le Mons, where the old Atheist, unable to pray, gives vent to his agonized feelings in a feeble attempt to trill out a few lines of a hymn — possibly the last fleeting reminiscence of an innocent childhood — and his fellow Bohemians, one with a dog on his lap, another with a violin in his fingers, and a third with a pack of cards half out of his pocket, humbly and solemnly joining in the strain — has for depth of feeling and grotesqueness scarce an equal in the whole range of English literature. — *Trübner's (London) Literary Record.*

*** This book is sold everywhere, and will be sent by mail, *postage free*, on receipt of price, $2.00.

G. W. CARLETON, Publisher,
497 BROADWAY, NEW YORK.

THE ORPHEUS C. KERR PAPERS.
FIRST, SECOND, AND THIRD SERIES.
3 VOLS. 12MO. CLOTH. PRICE $1.50 EACH.

These inimitable specimens of American Wit and Humor may be justly spoken of as world-renowned; for, in addition to their sale of upwards of fifty thousand copies in this country, there have been no less than four rival editions of them published in England. The following extracts from genuine criticisms show that the "PAPERS" enjoy the hearty commendation of the *highest critical authorities* in either country.

From the London Athenæum, in a three-column review.

"We opened his ('Orpheus C. Kerr's') volume with some misgiving, some dread lest wrong should be done to the honest who survived, or the brave who have gone down on either side in the great American struggle. We speedily, however, found ourselves reassured. Mr. Newell has, perhaps, an occasional hard hit at the Southerners; but, taken altogether, he is pretty impartial, and scatters his jokes wherever he finds anything that can justify him in flinging them about. The weaknesses, follies, eccentricities, blunderings, and vices of human nature, as exhibited by the smaller men in the late great struggle, are fair game for him, and probably no men will laugh more sincerely than those at whom Mr. Newell laughs most loudly himself. In short, he makes mirth out of that which affords so much food for mirth, in similar circumstances, here at home. . . . . . For prose, rhymes, parodies, and some good common sense uttered under the mask of satire, this volume may be commended to the notice of all holiday-makers this Christmas tide."

. . . The great success of the volumes of burlesque war-correspondence by "Orpheus C. Kerr" (Robert H. Newell) has placed him at the head of American humorists. Yet it would be doing him injustice to consider him as a mere jester. He is, rather, a keen satirist, who uses wit as the means of giving greater force to criticisms just and needful, and wider currency to thoughts of weight and value.—*New York Independent.*

. . . He seizes the acme of the ludicrous as directly as Crockett himself.—*Round Table.*

. . . The writer of the "Orpheus C. Kerr Papers" has struck an original vein of humor, and works it with decided effect.—*New York Evening Post.*

. . . The reader enjoys the vein of the author with a feeling akin to that with which the public revelled in the Pickwick Papers when they first appeared.—*Wilkes' Spirit.*

. . . We have laughed over some of Orpheus's letters until our sides ached with the pleasant emotion. Their wit and humor were so original and racy, and their broad burlesque so queer and good-natured, that we laughed even when we wished to be sober and serious.—*Providence Journal.*

. . . This humorous historian of the War ranks highest amongst the wits and satirists of America, and, since Thackeray died, has no living rival in the realm of English humorous literature.—*California Golden Era.*

. . . It is noticeable, too, that this author's eccentricities never degenerate into "slang;" his wit is always that of a scholar, and his satire that of a gentleman.—*New York Leader.*

. . . They (the "Papers") stir one up as carbonic acid gas will. They pull our sides out into jovial convexity.—*Milwaukie Sentinel.*

. . . Although they take a professedly comic view of men and things, the reader will detect an undercurrent of deep thought and even sorrowful reflection on the great events of the day, which render them particularly attractive and suggestive.—*New York Sun.*

. . . Among the good effects of the late war in America is the intercourse —social and intellectual—which it has promoted between the United States and England. This is abundantly proved by the quantity of American books of humor—for the most part in blazing red or yellow covers—which stare us in the face in all the booksellers' windows. Some are good; some bad. The good ones—including the "Bigelow Papers," the "Autocrat of the Breakfast Table," Artemus Ward, and the "Orpheus C. Kerr Papers"—are *very* good.—*London Star.* "Literature of 1865."

⁎⁎* These books are sold everywhere, and will be sent by mail, *postage free*, on receipt of price, $1.50, by

G. W. CARLETON, Publisher,
497 BROADWAY, NEW YORK.

A Catalogue of
BOOKS
ISSUED BY
CARLETON,
NEW YORK.

1868.

"*There is a kind of physiognomy in the titles of books no less than in the faces of men, by which a skilful observer will know as well what to expect from the one as the other.*"—BUTLER.

NEW BOOKS
And New Editions Recently Published by
CARLETON, Publisher,
NEW YORK.

N.B.—THE PUBLISHERS, upon receipt of the price in advance, will send any of the following Books by mail, POSTAGE FREE, to any part of the United States. This convenient and very safe mode may be adopted when the neighboring Booksellers are not supplied with the desired work. State name and address in full.

Victor Hugo.

LES MISÉRABLES.—The celebrated novel. One large 8vo volume, paper covers, $2.00 ; . . . cloth bound, $2.50
LES MISÉRABLES.—In the Spanish language. Fine 8vo. edition, two vols., paper covers, $4.00 ; . . cloth bound, $5.00
JARGAL.—A new novel. Illustrated. . 12mo cloth, $1.75
THE LIFE OF VICTOR HUGO.—By himself. . 8vo. cloth, $1.75

Miss Muloch.

JOHN HALIFAX.—A novel. With illustration. 12mo. cloth, $1.75
A LIFE FOR A LIFE.— . do. do. $1.75

Charlotte Bronte (Currer Bell).

JANE EYRE.—A novel. With illustration. 12mo. cloth, $1.75
THE PROFESSOR.— do. . . do. . do. $1.75
SHIRLEY.— . do. . do. . do. $1.75
VILLETTE.— . do. . do. . do. $1.75

Hand-Books of Society.

THE HABITS OF GOOD SOCIETY; with thoughts, hints, and anecdotes, concerning nice points of taste, good manners, and the art of making oneself agreeable. The most entertaining work of the kind. . . . . 12mo. cloth, $1.75
THE ART OF CONVERSATION.—With directions for self-culture. A sensible and instructive work, that ought to be in the hands of every one who wishes to be either an agreeable talker or listener. . . . . 12mo. cloth, $1.50
THE ART OF AMUSING.—Graceful arts, games, tricks, and charades, intended to amuse everybody. With suggestions for private theatricals, tableaux, parlor and family amusements. Nearly 150 illustrative pictures. . 12mo. cloth, $2.00

Robinson Crusoe.

A handsome illustrated edition, complete. 12mo. cloth, $1 50

Mrs. Mary J. Holmes' Works.

'LENA RIVERS.—	A novel.	12mo. cloth,	$1.50
DARKNESS AND DAYLIGHT.—	do.	do.	$1.50
TEMPEST AND SUNSHINE.—	do.	do.	$1.50
MARIAN GREY.—	do.	do.	$1.50
MEADOW BROOK.—	do.	do.	$1.50
ENGLISH ORPHANS.—	do.	do.	$1.50
DORA DEANE.—	do.	do.	$1.50
COUSIN MAUDE.—	do.	do.	$1.50
HOMESTEAD ON THE HILLSIDE.—	do.	do.	$1.50
HUGH WORTHINGTON.—	do.	do.	$1.50
THE CAMERON PRIDE.—	do.	do.	$1.50
ROSE MATHER.—*Just Published.*	do.	do.	$1.50

Miss Augusta J. Evans.

BEULAH.—A novel of great power.		12mo. cloth,	$1.75
MACARIA.— do. do.		do.	$1.75
ST. ELMO.— do. do. *Just Published.*		do.	$2.00

By the Author of "Rutledge."

RUTLEDGE.—A deeply interesting novel.		12mo. cloth,	$1.75
THE SUTHERLANDS.— do.		do.	$1.75
FRANK WARRINGTON.— do.		do.	$1.75
ST. PHILIP'S.— do.		do.	$1.75
LOUIE'S LAST TERM AT ST. MARY'S.—		do.	$1.75
ROUNDHEARTS AND OTHER STORIES.—For children.		do.	$1.75
A ROSARY FOR LENT.—Devotional Readings.		do.	$1.75

Captain Mayne Reid's Works—Illustrated.

THE SCALP HUNTERS.—	A romance.	12mo. cloth,	$1.75
THE RIFLE RANGERS.—	do.	do.	$1.75
THE TIGER HUNTER.—	do.	do.	$1.75
OSCEOLA, THE SEMINOLE.—	do.	do.	$1.75
THE WAR TRAIL.—	do.	do	$1.75
THE HUNTER'S FEAST.—	do.	do.	$1.75
RANGERS AND REGULATORS.—	do.	do.	$1.75
THE WHITE CHIEF.—	do.	do.	$1.75
THE QUADROON.—	do.	do.	$1.75
THE WILD HUNTRESS.—	do.	do.	$1.75
THE WOOD RANGERS.—	do.	do.	$1.75
WILD LIFE.—	do.	do.	$1.75
THE MAROON.—	do.	do.	$1.75
LOST LEONORE.—	do.	do.	$1.75
THE HEADLESS HORSEMAN.—	do.	do.	$1.75
THE WHITE GAUNTLET.— *Just Published.*		do.	$1.75

A. S. Roe's Works.

A LONG LOOK AHEAD.—	A novel.	12mo. cloth,	$1.50
TO LOVE AND TO BE LOVED.—	do.	do.	$1.50
TIME AND TIDE.—	do.	do.	$1.50
I'VE BEEN THINKING. —	do.	do.	$1.50
THE STAR AND THE CLOUD.—	do.	do.	$1.50
TRUE TO THE LAST.—	do.	do.	$1.50
HOW COULD HE HELP IT?—	do.	do.	$1.50
LIKE AND UNLIKE.—	do.	do.	$1.50
LOOKING AROUND.—	do.	do.	$1.50
WOMAN OUR ANGEL.—	do.	do.	$1.50
THE CLOUD ON THE HEART.—*Just Published.*		do.	$1.50

Orpheus C. Kerr.

THE ORPHEUS C. KERR PAPERS.—Three vols.	12mo. cloth,	$1.50
SMOKED GLASS.—New comic book. Illustrated.	do.	$1.50
AVERY GLIBUN.—A powerful new novel.—	8vo. cloth,	$2.00

Richard B. Kimball.

WAS HE SUCCESSFUL?— A novel.	12mo. cloth,	$1.75
UNDERCURRENTS.— do.	do.	$1.75
SAINT LEGER.— do.	do.	$1.75
ROMANCE OF STUDENT LIFE.—do.	do.	$1.75
IN THE TROPICS.— do.	do.	$1.75
HENRY POWERS, Banker.—*Just Published.*	do.	$1.75

Comic Books—Illustrated.

ARTEMUS WARD, His Book.—Letters, etc.	12mo. cl.,	$1.50
DO. His Travels—Mormons, etc.	do.	$1.50
DO. In London.—Punch Letters.	do.	$1.50
JOSH BILLINGS ON ICE, and other things.—	do.	$1.50
DO. His Book of Proverbs, etc.	do.	$1.50
WIDOW SPRIGGINS.—By author "Widow Bedott."	do.	$1.75
FOLLY AS IT FLIES.—By Fanny Fern.	do.	$1.50
CORRY O'LANUS.—His views and opinions.	do.	$1.50
VERDANT GREEN.—A racy English college story.	do.	$1.50
CONDENSED NOVELS, ETC.—By F. Bret Harte.	do.	$1.50
THE SQUIBOB PAPERS.—By John Phœnix.	do.	$1.50
MILES O'REILLY.—His Book of Adventures.	do.	$1.50
DO. Baked Meats, etc.	do.	$1.75

"Brick" Pomeroy.

SENSE.—An illustrated vol. of fireside musings.	12mo. cl.,	$1.50
NONSENSE.— do. do. comic sketches.	do.	$1.50

Joseph Rodman Drake.

THE CULPRIT FAY.—A faery poem.	12mo. cloth,	$1.25
THE CULPRIT FAY.—An illustrated edition. 100 exquisite illustrations. 4to., beautifully printed and bound.		$5.00

New American Novels.

TEMPLE HOUSE.—By Mrs. Elizabeth Stoddard. 12mo. cl., $1.75
THE BISHOP'S SON.—By Alice Cary. . . do. $1.75
BEAUSEINCOURT.—By Mrs. C. A. Warfield. . do. $1.75
HOUSEHOLD OF BOUVERIE. do. do. . do. $2.00
HELEN COURTENAY.—By author "Vernon Grove." do. $1.75
PECULIAR.—By Epes Sargent. . . . do. $1.75
VANQUISHED.—By Miss Agnes Leonard. . do. $1.75
FOUR OAKS.—By Kamba Thorpe. . . . do $1.75
MALBROOK.—*In press.* . . . . . do. $1.75

M. Michelet's Remarkable Works.

LOVE (L'AMOUR).—Translated from the French. 12mo. cl., $1.50
WOMAN (LA FEMME).— . do. . do. $1.50

Ernest Renan.

THE LIFE OF JESUS.—Translated from the French. 12mo.cl.,$1.75
THE APOSTLES.— . . do. . . do. $1.75

Popular Italian Novels.

DOCTOR ANTONIO.—A love story. By Ruffini. 12mo. cl., $1.75
BEATRICE CENCI.—By Guerrazzi, with portrait. do. $1.75

Rev. John Cumming, D.D., of London.

THE GREAT TRIBULATION.—Two series. 12mo. cloth, $1.50
THE GREAT PREPARATION.— do. . do. $1.50
THE GREAT CONSUMMATION. do. . do. $1.50
THE LAST WARNING CRY.— . . do. $1.50

Mrs. Ritchie (Anna Cora Mowatt).

FAIRY FINGERS.—A capital new novel. . 12mo. cloth, $1.75
THE MUTE SINGER.— do. . do. $1.75
THE CLERGYMAN'S WIFE—and other stories. do. . $1.75

Mother Goose for Grown Folks.

HUMOROUS RHYMES for grown people. . 12mo. cloth, 1 .25

T. S. Arthur's New Works.

LIGHT ON SHADOWED PATHS.—A novel. 12mo. cloth, $1.50
OUT IN THE WORLD.— . do. . . do. $1.50
NOTHING BUT MONEY.— . do. . . do. $1.50
WHAT CAME AFTERWARDS.— do. . . do. $1.50
OUR NEIGHBORS.— . do. . . do. $1.50

New English Novels.

WOMAN'S STRATEGY.—Beautifully illustrated. 12mo. cloth, $1.50
BEYMINSTRE.—By a popular author. . do. $1.75
"RECOMMENDED TO MERCY."— do. . . do. $1.75
WYLDER'S HAND.—By Sheridan Le Fanu. do. $1.75
HOUSE BY THE CHURCHYARD.— do. . do. $1.75

Edmund Kirke.

AMONG THE PINES.—Or Life in the South.   12mo. cloth, $1.50
MY SOUTHERN FRIENDS.—   do.   .   .   do. $1.50
DOWN IN TENNESSEE.—   do.   .   .   do. $1.50
ADRIFT IN DIXIE.—   do.   .   .   do. $1.50
AMONG THE GUERILLAS.—   do.   .   .   do. $1.50

Charles Reade.

THE CLOISTER AND THE HEARTH.—A magnificent new novel—the best this author ever wrote.   8vo. cloth, $2.00

The Opera.

TALES FROM THE OPERAS.—A collection of clever stories, based upon the plots of all the famous operas. 12mo. cloth, $1.50

Robert B. Roosevelt.

THE GAME-FISH OF THE NORTH.—Illustrated.   12mo. cloth, $2.00
SUPERIOR FISHING.—   do.   do. $2.00
THE GAME-BIRDS OF THE NORTH.—   .   .   do. $2.00

Hinton Rowan Helper.

THE IMPENDING CRISIS OF THE SOUTH.—   .   12mo. cloth, $2.00
NOJOQUE.—A Question for a Continent.   .   do. $2.00

Henry Morford.

PARIS IN '67.—Sketches of travel.   .   12mo. cloth, $1.75

From the German.

WILL-O'-THE-WISP.—A beautiful child's book.   12mo. cl., $1.50

The City of Richmond.

RICHMOND DURING THE WAR.—By a lady.   12mo. cloth, $1.75

Dr. J. J. Craven.

THE PRISON-LIFE OF JEFFERSON DAVIS.—Incidents and conversations during his captivity at Fortress Monroe. 12mo.cl.,$2.00

Captain Raphael Semmes.

THE CRUISE OF THE ALABAMA AND SUMTER.—   12mo. cloth, $2.00

John S. Mosby.

HIS LIFE AND EXPLOITS IN THE WAR.—With portraits.   do. $1.75

Walter Barrett, Clerk.

THE OLD MERCHANTS OF NEW YORK.—Personal incidents, sketches, bits of biography, and events in the life of leading merchants in New York City. Four series. 12mo. cl., $1.75

Madame Octavia Walton Le Vert.

SOUVENIRS OF TRAVEL.—New edition. Large 12mo. cloth, $2.00

H. T. Sperry.

COUNTRY LOVE vs. CITY FLIRTATION.—A capital new Society tale, with 20 superb illustrations by Hoppin. 12mo. cloth, $2.00

Miscellaneous Works.

MADEMOISELLE MERQUEM.—By George Sand.	12mo. cl.,	$1.75
LOVE IN LETTERS.—A fascinating collection.	do.	$2.00
A BOOK ABOUT LAWYERS.—From London edition.	do.	$2.00
LAUS VENERIS.—Poems by Algernon Swinburne.	do.	$1.75
OUR ARTIST IN CUBA.—By Geo. W. Carleton.	do.	$1.50
OUR ARTIST IN PERU.— do. do.	do.	$1.50
HOW TO MAKE MONEY, and How to Keep It.—	do.	$1.50
FAIRFAX.—A novel. By John Esten Cooke.	do.	$1.75
HILT TO HILT.— do. do.	do.	$1.75
THE LOST CAUSE REGAINED.—By Edw. A. Pollard.	do.	$1.50
MARY BRANDEGEE.—A novel. By Cuyler Pine.	do.	$1.75
RENSHAWE.— do. do.	do.	$1.75
THE SHENANDOAH.—History of the Conf. steamer.	do.	$1.50
MEMORIALS OF JUNIUS BRUTUS BOOTH.—(The Elder.)	do.	$1.50
MOUNT CALVARY.—By Matthew Hale Smith.	do.	$2.00
LOVE-LIFE OF DR. E. K. KANE AND MARGARET FOX.	do.	$1.75
BALLADS.—By the author of "Barbara's History."	do.	$1.50
MAN, and the Conditions that Surround Him.	do.	$1.75
PROMETHEUS IN ATLANTIS.—A prophecy.	do.	$2.00
TITAN AGONISTES.—An American novel.	do.	$2.00
PULPIT PUNGENCIES.—Witticisms from the Pulpit.	do.	$1.75
CHOLERA.—A handbook on its treatment and cure.	do.	$1.00
ALICE OF MONMOUTH.—By Edmund C. Stedman.	do.	$1.25
NOTES ON SHAKSPEARE.—By Jas. H. Hackett.	do.	$1.50
THE MONTANAS.—A novel. By Mrs. S. J. Hancock.	do.	$1.75
PASTIMES WITH LITTLE FRIENDS.—Martha H. Butt.	do.	$1.50
LIFE OF JAMES STEPHENS.—Fenian Head-Centre.	do.	$1.00
POEMS.—By Gay H. Naramore.	do.	$1.50
GOMERY OF MONTGOMERY.—By C. A. Washburn.	do.	$2.00
POEMS.—By Mrs. Sarah T. Bolton.	do.	$1.50
CENTEOLA.—By author "Green Mountain Boys."	do.	$1.50
RED-TAPE AND PIGEON-HOLE GENERALS—	do.	$1.50
TREATISE ON DEAFNESS.—By Dr. E. B. Lighthill.	do.	$1.50
AROUND THE PYRAMIDS.—By Gen. Aaron Ward.	do.	$1.50
CHINA AND THE CHINESE.—By W. L. G. Smith.	do.	$1.50
EDGAR POE AND HIS CRITICS.—By Mrs. Whitman.	do.	$1.00
MARRIED OFF.—An Illustrated Satirical Poem.	do.	50 cts.
THE RUSSIAN BALL.— do. do. do.	do.	50 cts.
THE SNOBLACE BALL.— do. do. do.	do.	50 cts.
THE CITY'S HEART. do. do. do.	do.	$1.00
POEMS.—By Mrs. Virginia Quarles.	do.	$1.00
AN ANSWER TO HUGH MILLER.—By T. A. Davies.	do.	$1.50
COSMOGONY.—By Thomas A. Davies.	8vo.	$2.00
RURAL ARCHITECTURE.—By M. Field. Illustrated.	do.	$2.00

www.ingramcontent.com/pod-product-compliance
Lightning Source LLC
Chambersburg PA
CBHW031328230426
43670CB00006B/274